A Guide to
Sources of
Information
in Libraries

A Guide to Sources of Information in Libraries

James G. Ollé

Gower   A Grafton Book

Published by
Gower Publishing Company Limited
Gower House Croft Road
Aldershot Hants GU11 3HR
and
Old Post Road
Brookfield
Vermont 05036
USA

Printed and bound in Great Britain by
Biddles Ltd, Guildford and King's Lynn

British Library Cataloguing in Publication Data

Ollé, James
   How to use information sources in libraries.
   1. Libraries and readers   2. Reference
   services (Libraries)   3. Information services
   I. Title
   025.5'2   Z710

   ISBN 0-566-03477-8

Library of Congress Cataloging in Publication Data

Ollé, James Gordon Herbert.
   How to use information sources in libraries.

   (A Grafton book)
   Includes bibliographical references and index.
   1. Reference services (Libraries)   2. Reference books.
   3. Library resources.   4. Library orientation.
   5. Bibliography—Methodology.   6. Research—Methodology.
   I. Title
   Z711.043 1984   025.5'2   84-4066
   ISBN 0-566-03477-8

Contents

Acknowledgements
List of abbreviations

Introduction: the pattern of sources of information   1

Part 1: The physical sources
Introduction   9
1   The printed word   11
2   Microforms   14
3   Audio: tapes and discs   18
4   Visual aids: films, film-strips and video   20
5   Videotex   22
6   Online   25
7   New media versus old media   31

Part 2: The literary sources
Introduction   37
8   Language dictionaries   38
9   Monographs   44
10   Encyclopedias   47
11   Yearbooks   53
12   Newspapers   55
13   Periodicals   59
14   Conference proceedings   65
15   Collections, festschriften and anthologies   66
16   Government publications   69
17   Statistics   74
18   Directories   78
19   Biographical sources of information   81
20   Geographical sources of information   85
21   Patent specifications and standards   92
22   Dictionaries of quotations and concordances   95

23 Illustrations   98
24 Printed ephemera   100
25 Theses (dissertations)   102

Part 3: The bibliographical sources
Introduction   107
26 Enumerative bibliography and bibliographic control   108
27 General national bibliographies   115
28 Published library catalogues   126
29 Bibliographies of periodicals   129
30 Bibliographic control of the contents of periodicals   133
31 Bibliographic control of the conference proceedings   144
32 Bibliographies of creative literature   146
33 Subject bibliographies   149
34 Literature guides   153
35 Author bibliographies   156
36 Records of research in process   160
37 The need for bibliographical literacy   161

Appendices
1   Principal sources of information on reference material   167
2   A note on copyright   171

Index   172

Acknowledgements

Although this book is based on many years experience in using reference material, first as a reference librarian in the public library service and latterly as a lecturer in library resources and assistance to readers at the schools of librarianship of Loughborough Technical College and Loughborough University of Technology, I would like to acknowledge the help I have received from the authors (most of them colleagues in the library profession) of various books and articles on particular types of sources of information. My debts to these authors have all been made clear, I hope, in the 'Further reading' sections at the ends of the individual chapters.

James G. Ollé
Loughborough, Leics.

List of abbreviations

The following abbreviations have been used throughout for the more important sources of information on reference material:

Ellis
Encyclopedia of library and information science, New York: Dekker, 1968–82. 33 vols, *Supplement*, 1983.

Grogan
Grogan, Dennis, *Science and technology: an introduction to the literature*, 4th edn, Bingley, 1982.

Higgens
Higgens, Gavin (ed.), *Printed reference material*, 2nd edn, Library Association, 1983.

Sheehy
Sheehy, Eugene P. (ed.), *Guide to reference books*, 9th edn, Chicago: American Library Association, 1976. *Supplement*, 1980.

Walford
Walford, A.J., *Guide to reference material*, Library Association, 1977–83, 3 vols. (The latest revised volumes are a mixture of the 3rd and 4th edns.)

Further information on these works will be found in Appendix 1, except for *Ellis*, which is described in chapter 10.

Introduction: the pattern of sources of information

Many years ago, a well-known librarian said 'A library consists of books, brains and a building', by which he meant stock, staff and accommodation. This was neither witty nor altogether wise. For one thing, there must be a fourth element, readers. Without them a library is a mere bibliosepulchre.

This manual is concerned with the first element, stock, more particularly with that part of it which provides information. 'Information' is a good example of what A.P. Herbert (Sir Alan Herbert) called 'witch words', words which have acquired biased meanings. Information, we are told on all sides, is essential to our progress and well-being. The implication is that all information is good. If librarians have any doubts about this in private, they seldom voice them in public.

But the term 'information' is too often used by librarians and information scientists when what they really mean is *bibliographic information*, thus confusing the means with the end. The dictionaries of the English language are more or less in accord as to the meaning of information: communicated facts or knowledge. In this manual, information will be taken to encompass not only facts (for example, the world is round) but ideas (for example, there may be life on other planets).

A point worth arguing, although it will not be argued here, is whether there should be any limits (ethical or economic) to the information libraries provide. My concern is with the variety and nature of the sources of information available today in, or through, libraries. I say through libraries, as most libraries obtain some of the information for which they are requested from other libraries and institutions. An increasing number obtain it from remote computerised databases or databanks.

The education of student librarians poses many difficulties. The worst part of the library school curriculum is what used to be called 'Library stock and assistance to readers'. For many years this demanded a close acquaintance with the 'best' reference works, details of which had to be learnt by

1

rote. The affect of this mode of study, which should have been foreseen, became progressively worse as the all-purpose general reference libraries became a dwindling minority, overtaken in numbers by special departments and special libraries.

Here we come to a fundamental fact about the present-day library scene: the variety of libraries which exist. Few library school students know, for sure, in what type of library they will work after they have graduated. Few reference sources are available in all libraries. (It would not be too daring to say 'No' instead of 'Few'.) The best thing a student can do, therefore, is to acquaint himself with the various ways in which information is stored and presented, so that at least he will know what to look for when he goes to work in an unfamiliar library, and will not be unduly puzzled by any kind of information package he may have to use.

The nature of the packages will depend partly upon their *physical form* and partly on their *literary form*. Physical forms were diverse even before the latest inventions of the information technologists appeared. Apart from manuscripts, and the varied forms of printed documents (readily apparent in any good collection devoted to local studies) we have had, for some years, auxiliary sources of information in libraries, such as photographic prints, slides and sound recordings. We now have several new physical forms whose only common factor is that they all need the use of electrical power.

By literary form I mean the way in which information expressed in words and figures is organised and presented. It could be as a continuous composition intended for progressive reading, or it could be organised according to some helpful scheme of arrangement for the swift retrieval of individual facts, as in a dictionary or encyclopedia.

It is not possible to make a neat, mutually exclusive list of information packages as straightforward as the table of British monarchs appended to W.C. Sellar and P.J. Yeatman's *1066 and all that*, where the Georges and Williams follow each other consecutively, an admirable mnemonic grouping which unfortunately history does not endorse.

The chapters which follow, in Parts I, II and III, reflect as clearly as possible the variety of sources of information librarians and library users must know, with the reservation that the pattern is not quite the same for every subject, or every library. Although I use the word 'pattern', as I have indicated, it is not clear-cut, and it is not possible to make it so. Librarians have no control over the sources of information they purchase or rent. But it should be recognised that the major difficulty in the way of producing a neat pattern of types of sources of information is not so much the intrusion of the new information media as the enduring problems associated with the old established printed and literary forms. The point can readily be demonstrated. Not all directory information is in directories. Not all maps are published separately, or are in atlases. Not all conference papers published are in the collected volumes of conference proceedings. Government publications are commonly regarded as a distinct type of sources of information, but they include monographs, directories, yearbooks, standards, research reports and audio-visual materials.

There is some hope that the new information media will eventually prove a blessing by overcoming the problems we have to endure of overlap and concealed information. In the meantime librarians must get to know the characteristics, that is to say, the virtues and defects of the various types of information sources. Knowledge of specific sources, printed and otherwise, will come, as required, by experience. But as to that, I am reminded of the late Dr S.R. Ranganathan, who once told an audience of young librarians 'When an experienced member of a library staff leaves that library he takes with him part of its memory.' This was said over thirty years ago, but it is still true. A library's catalogue always conceals more about the library's resources than it reveals.

But to return to the pattern of sources of information; a familiarity with this should be useful to a newly qualified librarian in any kind of library, as it should enable him to make an intelligent investigation of the stock and extramural resources and ask pertinent questions about them. Needless to say, what readers of this book will value most, and remember best, is what they discover for themselves. All I can do is to try to provide a map to assist their explorations. This brings me to the question of individual sources of information: which of them should be named and described in this book?

When G.K. Chesterton wrote his *Short history of England* (Chatto & Windus, 1917) he contrived to do so without providing a single date, or any other precise facts. Originally I intended to be equally drastic and discuss the various kinds of sources of information without mentioning any specific titles. Obviously, I have not kept to this intention. But for the most part, the individual sources of information named and described have been chosen only because I think they are good examples of their kind and worth examining. I do not mean to imply that any publication or database I mention should be stocked, or made accessible, in every library which provides an information service, or that the details of it should be memorised by every student librarian. Having said this, I must add that any reader of this manual who works in a library in the English-speaking world will find it useful to know some of the general bibliographies of books and periodicals dealt with in chapters 27 and 29.

Sooner or later the readers of this book will have to know intimately the major sources of information in the libraries they work in. How should these sources be assessed? In the older textbooks on reference material it was customary to provide a code of assessment, which, supposedly, could be applied to any reference work. No such code is offered here. Most of the criteria are too obvious to be stated and discussed, and others relate only to particular types of sources of information such as maps, bibliographies and online databases. These have been dealt with in the chapters on them.

There is, however, one point which should be mentioned here — 'up to dateness'. Librarians soon learn to become sensitive about the dates of the sources of information they provide. With some of the new media (for example, videotex) it is possible to be up to date in the sense of being correct up to the present day, or even the present hour. But in most libraries printed sources of information are predominant.

Broadly speaking, information in printed form is most up to date in the latest issues of newspapers and periodicals. Information in books is likely to be at least six months old when the book is new, except in a few popular yearbooks. Information which has taken some months to get into print is not necessarily superseded. The trouble is that a reader is probably unable to determine what is correct and what is incorrect.

When examining a book one must get behind the date of publication to discover the effective date of the information provided, the 'cut-off date' of the text. With luck the author may have been able to insert new information at the proof stage, and publication has quickly followed proof correction, but this cannot be depended upon. If a book is well documented, with numerous and precise references to other books, and, better still, to periodicals, the effective date of the text should be easy to determine.

Up to World War II there were several well-known London

publishers who refused to date their books. But in order to claim international copyright one must provide the date of publication, as well as the international copyright sign. It is unusual today for the date of publication to be withheld, except among non-commercial local publications.

With experience, librarians develop a remarkable flair for assessing the validity of sources of information, even on subjects with which they are not well acquainted. Partly this is due to their ever growing knowledge of authors and publishers, but partly also to trained observation, and a proper suspicion of the claims made by vendors of information, printed or other.

Part 1: The physical sources

Part 1: The physicist

Introduction

Until recently, the authors of manuals on reference and other information sources in libraries felt little need to pay particular attention to their physical nature, as the majority of the materials discussed were printed. But the situation is changing. It is true that printed sources still predominate, but others are becoming more varied, more obvious and certainly more important. In the following chapters on the physical pattern of information sources the printed forms are not ignored, but the accent is on the new media, their characteristics, advantages, disadvantages, and probable future.

1 The printed word

Although the introduction of printing from movable types, in the fifteenth century, caused a revolution in communication through written records, it was a long time before its full effect was felt by libraries. When the English monasteries were dissolved, in the 1530s, few printed books were found in their libraries, except at Syon, a late foundation. The formation of libraries of printed books did not become fashionable until the seventeenth century. Periodicals and newspapers did not become a significant part of library stocks until the latter part of the eighteenth century. Libraries themselves did not become numerous until the latter part of the nineteenth century when, in the larger towns, they became accessible to all classes of the community. It was not until then, when we had an organised library profession, that much attention was paid to basic library problems, such as the cataloguing of the stock and its arrangement on the shelves. But there were two problems rather more formidable and in dealing with these, libraries had to rely heavily on outside help. One was conservation, vitally important in libraries with research collections. (It is a major problem now in the British Library Reference Division). The other was finding information when it was wanted in books, pamphlets, periodicals, newspapers, and all the other forms in which the printed word appears. This is part of the eternal problem of information retrieval, still at its most challenging complexity in the realm of printed materials by virtue of their variety and their colossal number.

There is no point in trying to estimate the quantity of printed materials in the world today. No one knows for sure even the rough total. It is indicative of their bulk that the stocks of the great national research libraries are measured less often now by the number of volumes in stock than by the miles of shelving used to house them.

Librarians and library users have had to put up for so long with the many problems printed records have generated that one would expect them to welcome any reasonable alternatives which would reduce the labour of study, research and quick reference. Consider: a typical library of printed materials is one in which information is scattered not only by its literary forms, but by the variety of physical forms the printed word can assume. For almost any subject one can name, the distribution of printed sources in a library is likely to be, at the very least, a reference sequence, ordinary and oversize, a lending sequence, also ordinary and oversize, and a periodical collection. There may also be a stack for lesser used books and back files of periodicals, plus a number of boxes and cabinets for awkward materials such as pamphlets, maps and illustrations. There will be a catalogue, or catalogues of these, linked to the classification scheme used, but because the periodicals and newspapers, and also many of the books, will be miscellaneous in content, there will be a considerable amount of concealed information in the library which the catalogue and classification will not reveal. Some of this may be brought to light by the published bibliographies, such as indexing and abstracting services, to which the library subscribes. But a good deal of it will have to be searched for when required, which usually calls for time, knowledge and skill.

The new information media present their own problems, which include the cost and servicing of equipment (likely to be quickly superseded), coupled with the vexing problem of having to acquire multiple appliances because of incompatibility. But there are certainly advantages, as a few commonplace examples will show. Because *The Times* and the *Manchester Guardian* for the 1930s are on sale in microfilm, a research student at one of our new universities working on international reaction to the rise of Hitler will be able to do some of his work without migrating to an older library and there struggle with heavy bound volumes of the brittle originals. Because the library of Universal Chemicals Ltd has an online terminal, the tedious searching of shelves of printed volumes of *Chemical Abstracts* is unnecessary. (At Universal Chemicals it is recognised that time is money.) Because the Local Studies Department of Barchester City Libraries has acquired photographs and videotapes to augment the official reports of the local archaeological society on the recent excavation of a Roman barracks and granary on Eastgate Street, the frequent requests for information on this are handled with maximum efficiency.

It is generally conceded that print on paper will be with us for a long time yet, but as every library either already makes, or will soon have to make, some concessions to the new information media, it is important to consider their characteristics and what particular advantages they offer.

Further reading

Histories of printing abound, but from our point of view what matters most is not the technical detail but the impact of printing on the reading public. A splendid book to read on the development of a mass reading public in Britain from Caxton to the beginning of the present century, but with the accent on the nineteenth century, is Richard D. Altick, *The English common reader* (University of Chicago Press, 1957).

2 Microforms

Although microphotography was invented in the early days of photography, its practical uses were little explored until the 1930s. It was then that the systematic publishing of microforms of informational material began in the USA. Since then America has contributed a good deal to the development of microforms, as a recent history of them makes clear.[1]

First there was microfilm, but in 1944 the advantages of this were challenged by Fremont Rider, an American university librarian who had formerly been a publisher. He argued that it would be more convenient to have opaque microforms on cards of catalogue size. Following Rider's suggestion, microforms were actually manufactured according to his specification and marketed under the name of microcards.

Next there came from Holland another kind of transparent microform, the flat microfiche. Like the microcard it was easy to handle and store, but it was much easier to obtain from it a clear, sharp image. The invention of high reduction, computerised microfiches, and efficient machines to read them, have made microfiche, in recent years, the most popular of all microforms.

Unfortunately, libraries which need microforms in quantity for information and research, are obliged to stock all the types used by the microform publishers and provide the relevant reading machines, which are mostly incompatible. The characteristics and uses of the main types of microforms are as follows.

Transparent microforms

Microfilm

Despite its disadvantages, roll microfilm is still used extensively for copying files of periodicals and newspapers, and even entire collections of old books. Peter A. Thomas believes microfilm has no future, but among the publishers of microfilms is the British Library, evidently more optimistic.

Microfiche

A microfiche is a flat sheet of processed film. The standard A6 size, approximately 4 inches x 6 inches, will reproduce up to 98 pages in ordinary form. In computerised form (known as COM) it will reproduce up to 270 pages. Although microfiche can be used to copy all kinds of documents, microfilm is still preferred, on the whole, for newspapers and periodicals. A number of the larger libraries have lately transferred their own catalogues to computerised microfiche.

Opaque microforms

Microcard

The initial use of microcard was for the publication, immediately after World War II, of a back log of scientific research reports. Thereafter they were used for a variety of purposes, but for reasons mentioned below their use has declined.

Microprint

A Microprint (the term is a trade name of the Readex Microprint Corporation) is an opaque card 9 inches x 6 inches. The form has been used extensively for back files of American, British and United Nations official publications. Although they are still manufactured, Microprints, like microcards, have had to give way to the popular, versatile microfiche. The disadvantages of the opaque microforms are (a) they can only be read by powerful reflected light and (b) it is difficult to make satisfactory print-outs from them.

Few libraries can manage without some microforms. There are several reasons for this, although not all of them may apply to any particular library. The advantages are:

(a) Microforms save space. The saving can be considerable. In its original form a complete file of *The Times* weighs many tons and occupies considerable space. The entire microfilm edition can be unobtrusively accommodated in a few storage cabinets.

(b) The purchase of microform files of serials can overcome the inconvenience of the absence of original copies at the binders.

(c) Libraries can obtain the texts of many out-of-print publications of all kinds which could not be reprinted, or photocopied, economically.

(d)   The texts of documents such as theses and research reports of too limited interest to be published in printed form, even as facsimile typescripts, can be published easily and economically in microform.

(e)   Micro-facsimiles of unique manuscripts of historical and literary interest can be acquired by libraries in microfilm, or microfiche, in colour where necessary.

(f)   Libraries which hold rare publications, or unique manuscripts, can reduce or eliminate the handling of them by having microforms made for general use.

(g)   Substantial postal savings can be made on interlibrary loans by using microform copies instead of the originals. The British Library Lending Division lends many theses and research reports in microform.

The use of microforms, more especially of the transparent types, has been stimulated by the invention of reading machines which can print out photocopies of individual pages, and high speed photocopies which can produce quickly a Xerox copy of a complete book from a microfilm copy of it. For some years the firm of University Microfilms International has been able to supply, on demand, single copies of many out-of-print books of too little interest to attract the attention of reprint publishers.

It must be admitted that there are several disadvantages to microforms. They do not encourage either hopeful browsing or solid reading, and are therefore used rather grudgingly by some research workers in the humanities, whose laboratories are record repositories and research libraries. Also, using microforms it is difficult to cross-refer, to use simultaneously text and illustrations which appear on facing pages of the original documents, or to scan elaborate indexes. A further problem, complained of recently by Ann Niles, is the publication in microfilm of entire collections of documents without indexes to their contents.[2]

On the credit side, the technical quality of microforms is constantly improving, and research libraries founded in recent years can acquire, within their means, copies of a fair amount of research material which their readers could otherwise use only by travelling far afield.

It should be noted, however, that in the interests of students and researchers who do not wish to be tied to reading machines, some publications which have long been available in microform, such as *The Times Literary Supplement* and the major British government publications of the nineteenth century (notably the invaluable 'blue books') have been reprinted in facsimile in volume form in recent years.

The bibliographic control of microforms is hindered by the fact that they are not subject to the laws of legal deposit. A further complication is that not all microforms are published by the well-known microform publishers, of which there are comparatively few. Many learned societies and institutions (libraries among them) publish microforms also. The main source of information on published microforms is a massive, two-volume international catalogue: *Guide to microforms in print: author, title* and *Guide to microforms in print: subject* (Westport, Conn.: Meckler Publishing), revised annually.

Further reading

A writer to take note of in the microform field is S.J. Teague. His book *Microform librarianship* (2nd edn, Butterworths, 1979) is concise, lucid and authoritative. See also Teague's contribution to *The future of the printed word* edited by Philip Hills (Milton Keynes: Open University Press, 1980), chapter 10 'Microform publication'. There is also a good contribution by Virginia Carlson Smith to the *Art library manual* edited by Philip Pacey (Bowker, 1977) chapter 15 'Microforms'.

On recent developments see the *International Journal of Micrographics and Video Technology* (Pergamon Press) quarterly, successor to the rather more agreeable journal called *Microdoc.*

On the future of microforms, in addition to Teague's chapter see Peter A. Thomas 'Micropublishing and libraries in the future', *Aslib Proceedings*, **30** (5), May 1978, pp. 165–71.

References

1   Meckler, Alan, *A history of scholarly micropublishing in America 1938–1980*, (Westport, Conn.: Greenwood Press, 1982).
2   Niles, Ann, 'Bibliographic access for microform collections', *College and Research Libraries, 42* (6), November 1981, pp.576–80.

3 Audio: tapes and discs

One form of the new information technology librarians have not hesitated to make use of is sound recording on magnetic tape, especially since the invention of the audio cassette. Sound recordings on tape, reel-to-reel or cassette, have been used for several purposes in libraries, notably in language learning and in local studies. Audio cassettes have also been of great help to libraries providing services for the blind, although the production of talking newspapers for them, such as the excellent example at Deal, is largely done by volunteers.[1] In the USA selected reference works are being recorded on tape for the visually handicapped. The *World book encyclopedia*, for example, has been made available in 238 cassettes with Braille indexes.

Tape recording with cassettes has further stimulated the growth of oral history, in which libraries have played an important role. But like most sources of information, historical testimonies on audio tape must not be accepted uncritically. Bernard Crick's observation on this matter is worth considering:

> The past is filtered through what one subsequently learns. Memories are extremely valuable evidence, but they are not history in themselves. I'm all for oral history, so long as people don't think that its authenticity makes it true: it is only part of the evidence.[2]

On the other hand, Paul Thompson has said:

> The photograph has created a new type of visual history, compelling, but in its human message enigmatic. The voice is explicit. Its use changes not only the texture of history, but its content. It shifts the focus from laws, statistics, administrations, and governments, to people.[3]

Gramophone records were little used for recording the spoken word until the introduction of microgroove long-playing records in the 1950s. Since then they have been used with great success for literary recordings — poets such as Dylan Thomas and Sir John Betjeman reading their own works, and famous actors recording classic plays, including the entire Shakespeare canon. Long-playing records have also been widely used for language teaching, but they are now giving way to tapes.

In March 1983 the first high fidelity laser-scanned audio discs (known as compact discs, as they are only 12 cms in diameter) were released in the UK by Philips. It seems unlikely that compact discs will be used for the spoken word until the market for them has been built up with musical recordings, but this new medium has attractive possibilities. High quality, long-playing, durable sound recordings, protected from dust and needle-scratch, would be welcome in support of several areas of study — history, languages, literature and ornithology, for example.

Another important recent event in the audio field was the transfer of the British Institute of Recorded Sound to the British Library in April 1983. It has since been renamed the National Sound Archive, from which we may expect an authoritative national discography.

References

1   Holyoake, Gregory, 'Deal's talking newspaper', *Lady, 197* (5101), 17 March 1983, pp.520–1, 524.
2   Crick, Bernard, 'Orwell and biography', *London Review of Books, 4* (18), 7 October 1982, p.23.
3   Thompson, Paul, *The voice of the past: oral history*, Oxford University Press, 1978, p.223.

4 Visual aids: films, film-strips and video

Some information cannot be conveyed adequately by words alone. Librarians do not have to be told this and as pointed out in chapter 23, some public libraries took the trouble to build up collections of mounted illustrations many years ago. Since then the term 'visual aids' has come into use, calling to mind the 'resource centres' which have been provided over the past twenty years in our schools, as part of, or in addition to the school libraries.

The commercial and institutional production of visual and audio aids to education has become so substantial that the British Library has felt it necessary to compile and publish a special 'bibliography' of them, the *British catalogue of audiovisual materials*, the first 'experimental' edition of which was published by the Bibliographic Services Division in 1979. But it does not cover the whole range of visual aids. It excludes films and video tapes and video discs. 'Video' calls for comment as it is new and thriving.

Video tapes came on the market first and by the time video discs appeared the tapes had achieved a remarkable degree of popularity. Video tapes have disabilities. There are rival, incompatible systems, and unlike audio tapes they cannot be easily edited. But they have one great advantage over video discs: people can use blank tapes to make their own video recordings. They cannot record on video discs.

Both tapes and discs have considerable potential value as sources of information, if properly used. The educational value of tapes has been recognised by the Open University and the BBC (through BBC Enterprises). The value of video discs remains to be seen. Their advantages are not only the high quality of their sound and vision but the ability of the Laser Vision player to find and hold any particular frame.

But doubts have been expressed about the educational value of all visual and audiovisual aids in themselves, that is, unsupported by the printed word. The point has been well expressed in a leading article in the *Daily Telegraph*:

> Never mind that they only read comics and can't multiply by ten, cry the teachers; youth understands

visually and communicates orally. Several can operate computers. It should be replied bluntly that visual 'knowledge' is not knowledge. Bertrand Russell distinguished between the ostensive and verbal definitions of objects by asking: a matchbox, what is it? The ostensive reply is to point to one. The verbal reply is 'a container that holds matches'. One has not understood the nature of an object or concept until one can state it verbally. We stifle such ability among our children at our peril.[1]

The value of visual aids in libraries, as distinct from resource centres, is hardly a matter for argument.

Further reading

See the recent issues of the *Audiovisual Librarian*, quarterly journal of the Library Association and Aslib Audiovisual Groups.

References

1 'Now read on, if you can', *Daily Telegraph*, 25 July 1983, p.10.

5 Videotex

The most striking information technology innovations in the 1970s were the videotex systems. Although their reception by the general public has not matched the expectations of their promoters, by 1983 the simpler and cheaper teletext services, encouraged by the television rental firms, were gaining users. But the more sophisticated viewdata services were still recruiting only a small number of subscribers.

The terms and trade names in these new media are widely used, but less widely understood.

Videotex is an omnibus term which covers the one-way broadcast computerised information systems and the interactive systems which operate via the telephone network. The common denominator in all these systems is a television screen.

Teletext is the broadcast form of videotext. A television receiver, with additional circuits, reconstructs on its screen, in words and stylised illustrations, information which has been fed into a central computer. The information can be displayed on the screen alone, or superimposed over normal television pictures. An advantage of superimposition is that selected television programmes can be given captions, for optional use, to assist the hard of hearing. The BBC teletext service is called CEEFAX; the ITV and Channel 4 service is called ORACLE. These provide a mixed service of news, games and captions. The information services they provide may be used more often than the viewdata services, but they are much narrower in scope.

Viewdata is the term commonly used in the UK for interactive videotex, a two-way system using telephone links which enable users to transmit information as well as to receive it. (A much vaunted facility for the near future is 'tele-shopping'.) The major service in the UK (it was the first in the world) is British Telecom's PRESTEL. The recent extension to PRESTEL, by which subscribers can gain access to outside computers, is called GATEWAY.

When PRESTEL was launched, in 1979, the Post Office, which had developed it, but had not yet handed it over to

British Telecom, advertised it as 'a product with mass market appeal — highly relevant to both the business and residential markets'. The initial target was 50,000 subscribers by 1980. But by the end of 1982 there were only 21,000, and only about 3,000 of these were 'residential'. The majority of users were business subscribers. PRESTEL has been described by the *Financial Times* as 'a solution in search of a problem'.

PRESTEL's greatest success so far has been with the tourist industry, where up-to-date timetables and information on hotel vacancies, with immediate booking facilities, have been much appreciated.

The directory of PRESTEL's 'information providers' shows that it has tried to cater for too many needs and interests at once. This has been realised and the service will now be aimed at specific types of user. In other words the present sales strategy is 'segmenting the market'.

The experimental use of PRESTEL in libraries, one of the many forward-looking activities of the British Library, has had only a modest success. But it must be remembered that, so far, the system has used only about a quarter of its capacity of one million frames. Among the kinds of information libraries have found useful are parliamentary news, HMSO's list of new publications, economic and social statistics and the various kinds of directory information.

Although PRESTEL, like CEEFAX and ORACLE, uses a television screen, because it also uses the telephone network, every minute of use has to be paid for. The instant popularity of video (video recorders using videotapes) which involve, for prerecorded tapes, high rental charges, shows that, in their homes, people are far more eager to pay for the benefits of the new technology when they concern entertainment than when they relate to information. There should be nothing surprising about this; it is in accord with the weekly television ratings.

British Telecom's directory of PRESTEL's information providers (which should be examined), together with news of videotext around the world, will be found in the quarterly *PRESTEL User*.

Librarians have mixed feelings about videotex. It has great potential, but it will take some time to make it a commonplace aid to obtaining information. Apart from the 'pay-as-you-use' deterrent to the 'residential' use of viewdata, there is an overall difficulty with videotex: only a small amount of information can be shown on a television

23

screen, and although it is technically possible to provide high quality illustrations, the cost of doing so is at present prohibitive. Print-out facilities, which can be extremely useful for certain types of information (for example, statistical and timetable) are available, but fairly expensive.

There are a number of private viewdata services in commerce and industry which need not be surveyed here. But there is a local semi-public service of great interest. This is KINGTEL, operated by Kingston-on-Thames Public Libraries for the public and local councillors. The latter have a 'protected service'.

Further reading

There is already a substantial literature on videotex, but none of it is worth mentioning specifically as the situation is too fluid. Recent developments are reported from time to time in the *Library Association Record* and *Aslib Proceedings*. British Telecom publishes ample publicity material on PRESTEL.

6 Online

'Online' means interactive access to computerised stores of information. If the information stored is purely bibliographical the store is called a *database*. If the information is substantive (non-bibliographical) it is called a *databank*.

There is no need to provide here basic technical information on online. This is now widely available and has become an essential part of the curriculum of every school of librarianship. Online was pioneered in the USA by the Chemical Abstracts Service and the National Library of Medicine, publisher of the *Index Medicus*. Once computers were used in the processing of these well-known serial bibliographies it was soon realised that it would be an advantage to subscribers if they had direct access to the computerised databases, which were not only more up to date than the printed versions, but searchable with greater speed and ease. There was also a third advantage: the quick and accurate result of a search via a computer terminal could be immediately printed out. Within a decade, a new information retrieval industry based on computers grew up, bringing with it its own terminology to swell the already substantial glossary of librarianship. A notable feature of online, which has ceased to surprise, is that it crosses boundaries. It is not yet universal, but it is certainly transcontinental. It has brought to libraries new resources, and also new problems.

The benefits of online are undoubtedly great. As Dennis Grogan has said, it has 'placed an important new tool in the librarian's hands'. Remote, comprehensive and up to date computerised stores of information can be searched with 'hardware' (a telephone, keyboard, visual display unit and a printer) which need only a fraction of the space necessary for the published versions of the bibliographies and other reference works accessible online. Some of the published versions would be uneconomic to have in stock anyway, owing to limited use. Furthermore, in some subjects information is available online which has no published equivalent.

Online is used mainly for access to bibliographic databases, such as *Chemical Abstracts*, the *Zoological Record* and the *British Education Index*. But although many of the major serial bibliographies, notably the abstract and indexing services, are online, there is still a wealth of published bibliographical information which is not. It is unlikely that all of it ever will be. It is a question of the nature and volume of demand in relation to cost. For example, there are quite a number of useful small-scale bibliographies in the humanities (some of them of purely local material) which are never likely to attract the online entrepreneurs. According to Maurice B. Line, Director of the British Library Lending Division, 'Computer-based bibliographic searches generate only a small minority (one-seventh or one-eighth) of document requests'.[1] An Aslib survey of libraries with online terminals, carried out in 1982, showed that most of them answered less than 150 enquiries a year by online searches.

Bibliographic databases are not usually accessible through the publishing firms that generate them, but from vending organisations called 'hosts', who have acronymic names such as DIALOG, DIALTECH and BLAISE. BLAISE, the British Library Automated Information Service, is the most important British host. Since 1982 it has operated as two separate services, BLAISE-LINE, which covers several notable American abstracting/indexing files, including MEDLINE and CHEMLINE, and BLAISE-LINK, which covers the MARC (Machine Readable Cataloguing) files of the *British National Bibliography* and the Library of Congress, and also the *Eighteenth Century Short-Title Catalogue (ESTC)*. Registered users of the British Library Lending Division can forward, *via* BLAISE, requests to borrow documents listed in its files.

The searching of online bibliographic databases, which is not only quicker but likely to be more thorough than manual searching, has stimulated in libraries requests for photocopies, inter-library loans, and translations. But from a reader's point of view there are potential dangers, aggravated when the references cited are without abstracts, and aggravated still more if the reference interview, and the resultant search, have not been skilfully performed. This point has been well illustrated by Roy Davies:

> Having obtained a print-out of references the reader
> must then attempt to winnow the wheat from the chaff
> — not always an easy process, particularly if the data-
> bases concerned do not include abstracts. Some refer-
> ences which appear relevant may be in languages un-

26

familiar to the reader who must then decide whether or not to undertake another, probably manual, search to find out if translations exist and, if not, whether to commission translations. Next, having decided which references to follow up, the reader has to find out which of the items are available in his own library, which can itself be a time-consuming task. Some documents which the library is supposed to have may be on loan, mis-shelved, lost or even stolen. Items not available have to be requested through the inter-library loans service which introduces another, variable delay.[2]

The last point mentioned by Davies draws attention to a long-standing problem which has been highlighted by the increasing use of bibliographic databases — the delays which often occur in obtaining copies of documents requested as the result of online searching. This old problem has a new name: document delivery. Its exact nature, and what may be done to cope with it over the next decade, were ably discussed by Maurice B. Line at an Aslib conference on document delivery held in November 1982. As Mr Line pointed out, what the user needs is a quick and consistently reliable service, copies of documents in acceptable form (with particular care over high quality illustrations), the ability to assess content and quality before ordering, and all at little or no cost to himself![3]

What is hoped for is a series of developments in the transmission media acceptable to all concerned. A good discussion point is the probable effect of sophisticated electronic document transmission on publishers, particularly publishers of periodicals. Will some articles be withheld from formal publication and be available only on demand by transmission?

Although most information available online is bibliographical, over the past few years there has been useful progress in the formation of databanks. Some are numeric, that is, they provide statistical information. But to a limited extent text is also available. In the USA several well-known encyclopedias are now online, although with limitations. The full text of an encyclopedia may not be available, or the online service may not be available to libraries, which probably does not matter very much. The most outstanding examples of databanks so far, and an encouraging pointer to the way ahead, is to be found in the area of current legal information.

American lawyers have enjoyed the aid of computers for several years. But since 1980 there has been a successful British system, LEXIS (Butterworth Telepublishing Ltd), a full-text online information service on British law reports, to which there will shortly be added the texts of all current Statutes and Statutory Instruments. The tedium of searching bound volumes and copying from them (there is an optional print-out service for LEXIS, as well as a visual display unit) will soon be ended in legal offices. An interesting feature of LEXIS is that lawyers are willing to be instructed in how to use the system themselves. The sources of the law probably lend themselves better than the primary literature of other professions to this kind of treatment, but comparable online services for other professions will undoubtedly follow.

Since the mid-1970s, by which time a number of important bibliographic databases had become accessible in Britain, online terminals have become an accepted feature of many libraries where the information service justifies it. University and industrial special libraries are well to the fore, but with help and encouragement from the British Library a number of public libraries have also gone online. This means that we have now reached the stage where librarians can speak about online with their own authority. The matters librarians most particularly like to talk about are these:

(a) Which library users should be given the benefits of online? In academic libraries preference is likely to be given to the teaching and research staff and post-graduate research students.

(b) The expense of online searches, and to what extent enquirers should pay for them. It should be remembered here that the overall cost of manual searches can be appreciable; in some instances online searches could be cheaper. (The British Library Science Reference Library charges according to 'the time used on the computer and the number of references printed'.)

(c) Who should be allowed to use the online terminal? Enquirers (unhappily called, in the proliferating online jargon, 'end-users') are seldom allowed to, and are unlikely to be able to economically and efficiently. It should also be said that not all the members of library staffs make good online searchers.

(d) The problem of 'document delivery' mentioned above. This has been called by one librarian the 'document bottleneck'.

So far, online has been of the greatest benefit to research workers and practitioners in science, technology, medicine and some of the social sciences, notably law. Those whose interests are in one or other of the humanities are likely to be indifferent to online. This does not mean that the humanities have been altogether overlooked. *Historical Abstracts* are online. So is the *Eighteenth-Century Short-title Catalogue*. But the simple fact is — and it is hardly surprising — that the subjects covered best by online are those which were, and still are, well covered by printed information sources.

Although the future of online is not clear, it is promising. The only probable brakes on its development are economic, and the necessity for aptitude and training in the use of online terminals. The British Library pamphlet *Searching ESTC on BLAISE-LINE*, which is addressed to researchers in the humanities, says cheerfully:

> The BLAISE-LINE system is sophisticated and powerful, and mastering it requires patience and experience. However, the perceptive reader, once he has overcome the understandable difficulties in coming to terms with 'indexing', 'search qualifiers', 'logical operators' and the like, should quickly[!] grasp the ways in which computerised data opens [sic] a window on the past which traditional research tools have never provided.[4]

The growth of online systems is more likely to encourage than deter the use of the printed word. Even databanks will have their limitations, with facts more common than opinions. What A.J.P. Taylor has said about the facts of history can be applied to other subjects: 'Facts are not history, just as a skeleton is not a man. They are the raw material which the historian shapes into a pattern'.[5]

Further reading

The literature on online is already substantial, but much of it is technical or promotional. Furthermore, progress is so rapid that much of it is quickly outdated. However, a few things are worth mentioning.

The best starting point is Dennis Grogan, *Practical reference work* (Bingley, 1979) pp.46—8, 101—7). After this see *Higgens*, chapter 20, 'On-line information retrieval systems' by B. Houghton and the online symposium in the *Assistant Librarian*, 75 (1), January 1982.

A standard reference work in the field which should be examined is *Online bibliographic databases* by James L. Hall and Marjorie J. Brown (3rd edn, Aslib, 1983) which gives full details, including print-out samples, of 179 bibliographic databases of particular value to librarians and other information searchers. Although this directory is selective, the databases included offer access to nearly 80 million references. The helpful *Introduction* is worth reading in full.

For details of the online full-text retrieval systems providing legal information (LEXIS, EUROLEX and so on) see the recent issues of the *Law Librarian*.

References

1   Line, Maurice B., 'Document delivery, now and in the future', *Aslib Proceedings*, 35 (4), April 1983, p.167.
2   Davies, Roy, 'Documents, information or knowledge? Choices for librarians', *Journal of Librarianship*, 15 (1), January 1983, p.48.
3   Line, Maurice B., op. cit., pp.167–75.
4   Alston, R.C., *Searching ESTC on BLAISE-LINE*, British Library, 1982, (*Factotum* Occasional Paper 1) p.5.
5   Taylor, A.J.P., Foreword to *Dictionary of world history*, Nelson, 1973, p.XXI.

7   New media versus old media

That there will be a number of radical changes in the pattern of library resources and the nature of library methods before the end of the century is hardly worth saying. The extent of these changes is another matter.

The main topic of discussion with regard to the storage, retrieval and communication of information is the future of the printed word. But prognostications on its eclipse by other media are not altogether new. In August 1894, in the early days of the gramophone (phonograph), *Scribner's Magazine* published an article called 'The end of books' which predicted that printing would be replaced by 'phonography', libraries would be transformed into 'phonographotechs' and authors would become their own publishers.[1] In December 1932, Stephen Gaselee, librarian of the Foreign Office, told the members of the Bibliographical Society:

> It is by no means certain that the printed book will remain as the chief medium of the transmission of knowledge. The development of gramophones, broadcasting and television, or a combination of any two or all three of them, may eventually abolish the book except as a curiosity and a subject of antiquarian research.[2]

In the early 1960s, when microforms were becoming familiar, their keenest advocates set no bounds on their forecasts of their uses in libraries, and outside them. Dr R.S. Schultze, librarian of the Research Department of Kodak, told a bemused audience of library school students at Loughborough that before long people would not read the pages of books awkwardly with the aid of tables and chairs but comfortably by reading projected images of pages on walls and ceilings. This method of reading is not unknown, but it belongs more to hospitals and nursing homes than libraries and private dwellings. About the same time, Robert L. Collison, chief librarian of the BBC, said that, thanks to microfilm, every branch public library would soon be able to have all the reference works listed in *Walford* and *Winchell*. Enthusiasm for a new medium of communication could hardly go further.

Admittedly, the situation today is different. We now have several new media to consider and contend with. Even while we are trying to understand the technicalities and assess the vaunted benefits of one, along comes another, and yet another; and each one develops and changes, so that appliance/system Mark I is soon superseded by appliance/system Mark II; and medium X, which seemed so promising last year is threatened this year by medium Y; and so on.

A recent glimpse of new wonders of information technology shortly to bless us emanates from the British government's firm promise of the inauguration of multi-channel television to subscribing members of the public *via* house-to-house cables. Cable television was pioneered in the USA, where it is now widely used, although it has yet to reach every major city. In the UK it exists at present only in small experimental systems, but it is expected that, by 1984, several local cable television companies will be operating. In June 1983, the newly elected British government announced that it would shortly appoint a cable television authority to award franchises to cable television companies. The way for cable television has been prepared by the *Hunt Report* (October 1982), the report of a small committee appointed by the government, and a White Paper (April 1983) which endorsed the committee's recommendations.[3]

Cable television is mentioned for the reason, which may or may not be cogent, that the British government is committed to encourage the use of cable television for purposes other than entertainment, but what this promise is worth nobody knows. Information and instruction are hardly likely to rival the public's insatiable demand for entertainment. (On this see the illuminating 'Research' feature on the use made of the four 'off the air' television channels published weekly in the *Listener*.) What is feared by some of the television critics is that the new cable channels will follow the market leaders, so that instead of more choice there will be only more duplication.

But before becoming involved in the debate on the future of the information media, readers of this book are advised to go back a little in time and read three other books which, in different ways, try to relate the past to the future in the realm of information sources.

In decreasing order of interest the books I have in mind are, first: *The future of the printed word*, edited by Philip Hills, Milton Keynes: Open University, 1980. This is an excellent, well-planned symposium in which twelve experts drawn from the allied worlds of publishing, computer technology, librarianship and information science put their knowledge and opinions at the reader's disposal with good sense and lucidity.

If any single chapter may be particularly recommended it is chapter 2 'Some questions concerning the unprinted word' by Maurice B. Line, Director-General, British Library Lending Division. Among the several good points made by Mr Line are these:

1. Electronic storage and access is 'economically inevitable' for documents with a small readership, such as research papers.
2. Computer screens are not ideal either for scanning or continuous reading.
3. It is easier to refer to several documents at the same time in printed rather than in electronic form.
4. Electronic media are less useful than the printed word in the underdeveloped countries.

The second book is by James Thompson, *The end of libraries*, Bingley, 1982. The tone of this book is indicated by its title. The author, librarian of the University of Reading, argues earnestly that 'Technological progress has produced a pre-emptive technology which in due time will displace the larger part of mankind's present book-centred communal memory' (p.118). If one places the accent on the phrase 'in due time', Mr Thompson may be right. It is only fair to add that several distinguished publishers and librarians are not at all pessimistic about the future of the printed word.

The third book recommended is *The impact of new technology on libraries and information centres*, Library Association, 1982. This is the report of a Library Association working party. Its chief merit is that it provides a plain, structured review of the present situation in a short space. It is rather cautious about the future, but for this it can hardly be blamed. The principal point made is that 'the options open to the librarian for the provision of services to his users are increasing. They include remote retrieval systems, inhouse software packages, use of bureau services, microcomputers, shared cataloguing systems and office technology' (p.35). As to the future, the report can do little more than point to the problem of getting information from information 'systems' which are not 'user friendly' (the authors of the report are well acquainted with the jargon of the new information technology) and who will pay for the provision of information obtained at some cost from extramural sources in libraries where the information services are traditionally free.

An event which has taken place since these three books were published which may not be of major importance, but is hardly surprising, was the foundation, in the Spring of 1983, of an Information Technology Group of the Library Association. Jenny Rowley has objected to this, on the grounds that the developments in, and implications of information technology should be the concern of all Library Association members, and the existence of this new Group will encase discussion within it.

For the time being, let the last word be with John M. Strawthorn, one of the contributors to *The future of the printed word*, who said:

> We need to learn how best to get information out of one person's head and into another's. We need to know whether to use the printed word, some other kind of visual display, another medium of presentation (aural, tactile or olfactory), or a combination of these. (p.24).

Further reading

Although not so comprehensive as *The future of the printed word, Books on-line* (National Book League for Libtrad, 1981), the proceedings of a conference organised by the Working Party of Libraries and the Book Trade, is worth looking at. See especially 'Is there anyone in the library not working for the computer?' by Peter Lewis, pp.18–41. For a good-humoured criticism of information technology see Godfrey Thompson 'A view from the outside', *Audiovisual Librarian, 8* (2), Spring 1982, pp.62–6.

References

1   Uzanne, Octave, 'The end of books', *Scribner's Magazine*, August 1894, has been reprinted in *Printing History, 1* (2) 1979, pp.23–32.
2   Gaselee, Stephen, 'The aims of bibliography', *The Library*, 4th series, vol. *13* (3), December 1932, p.243 note.
3   Home Office, *Report of the inquiry into cable expansion and broadcasting policy*, Cmnd. 8679 (HMSO, 1982), Hunt Report.

Part 2: The literary sources

Introduction

In this part of the book we are dealing with sources of information which are mainly printed and are often called 'reference works' or 'non-bibliographical reference works'. Neither of these terms is likely to be used with absolute precision. To begin with, bibliographies are mainly reference works and quite a number of non-bibliographical reference works *include* bibliographies, (for example, large-scale encyclopedias) for which there is a very good term: 'concealed bibliographies'.

It is difficult to make a logical progression in ordering the chapters in this section, but we begin with the more familiar types of reference sources and end with the less familiar. In the beginning there had to be words, so we start with language dictionaries.

8   Language dictionaries

An office may get by with one dictionary, but even a small library will have to have several. Firstly, there must be not only English dictionaries but a few foreign language dictionaries — translating dictionaries anyway. Secondly, there must be enough varieties of each kind of dictionary to suit all the library's readers. We are fortunate in that most of the dictionaries we need can be obtained from a small number of British and American publishers who have high reputations in the lexicographical field. Difficulties arise when one has to buy imported dictionaries for minor foreign languages.

Dictionaries differ according to the range of words they define and the kinds of information they give about each word. Both factors are governed by the users the dictionaries are intended for. The larger the scope the more expensive a dictionary is to produce and keep up to date, although the use of computers is now going to be of help in producing new editions. It is very expensive to launch a new, high quality dictionary. *Collins dictionary of the English language* (1979) involved £1 million investment.

There is a tendency for popular dictionaries to become more informative, but they usually economise on matters only of interest to students of philology, such as etymology.

The main types of dictionaries, with notable examples, are as follows.

Dictionaries for general use

Defining

By this is meant general purpose dictionaries which exclude proper names, obsolete and dialectal words and deal lightly with slang and abbreviations. The *Concise Oxford dictionary* is perhaps the best-known, although it now has several new rivals which have been well received, notably the *Collins dictionary of the English language*, which provides very clearly an extraordinary amount of information in a handy single volume, and the *Longman new universal dictionary* (Longman, 1982) which is also a most impressive newcomer.

Encyclopedic

An encyclopedic dictionary incorporates some of the features of a small-scale encyclopedia. It has entries for famous people and institutions and also important places. It defines terms in the arts and sciences with illustrations where they seem necessary. This type of dictionary appeared rather late in Britain. A pioneer example, now called *The new Oxford illustrated dictionary* (Oxford University Press, two volumes, 1978) was first published in 1962. This type of dictionary has long been familiar in France (the Larousse series) and the USA.

Abbreviations

There are now so many abbreviations that we undoubtedly need separate dictionaries of them. They should also include acronyms. (An acronym is a 'word' formed from the initial letters of other words, e.g. NATO.) Unfortunately the creation of new abbreviations, especially of new societies and institutions, is faster than the dictionary makers can keep pace with. They are all too evident in librarianship and information science.

Dictionaries for special use

Learners'

A term for dictionaries aimed at foreign students of a language. They are particularly difficult to compile and some have been damned by reviewers. A very good example is the *Oxford advanced learner's dictionary of current English* (3rd edn, Oxford University Press, 1974).

Historical

An historical dictionary goes beyond etymology and indicates how words have been used since they entered the language by citing examples. The classic work of this type is the massive *Oxford English dictionary*, (Oxford: Clarendon Press), corrected reprint, 13 vols., 1933; *Supplement* A—Scz., 3 vols., 1972—82, in progress. The unusual bulk of this dictionary is explained by the fact that it uses over two million quotations to demonstrate changing usage. It was originally called *A new English dictionary on historical principles*. As its authority is such that it is sometimes used in the law courts, the publication of the new *Supplement* has been greatly welcomed.

Slang

The ordinary English dictionaries cannot cope with the wealth of slang. Much slang is jargon peculiar to certain occupations. The classic example of a slang dictionary is Eric Partridge, *A dictionary of slang and unconventional English*, (Routledge, 2 vols., 1970). A new edition, revised by Paul Beale, is due in 1984. Partridge said that this work was designed 'to form a humble companion to the monumental *Oxford English Dictionary*'.

Dialect

Most dictionaries of dialect deal with the dialect of particular regions (for example, Cornwall), but there is a standard general work: Joseph Wright, *English dialect dictionary* (Frowde, 6 vols., 1898–1905).

Subject

There are many dictionaries of terms used in particular trades and professions — nautical, theatrical and so on. The British example for librarianship is larger than one would expect. This is because it includes, quite reasonably, terms in printing, publishing and other fields peripheral to librarianship. The work in question is Leonard Montague Harrod, *The librarian's glossary and reference book* revised by Ray Prytherch (5th edn., Aldershot: Gower, 1983).

Glossaries

A glossary is a dictionary of words (regional, dialectal or obsolete) not part of present-day standard English. It is usually applied to a list at the end of a textbook, or an edition of a classic author (for example, Chaucer). But the term is not always used in this sense. Occasionally it is used for a separately published dictionary of specialised interest, or even for a textbook list of current terms used in a subject.

Synonyms

Coupled with antonyms (an antonym is a term which is opposite in meaning to another term) there are more than enough synonyms to make a large dictionary, see *Webster's new dictionary of synonyms* (Springfield, Mass.: Merriam, 1978).

Thesauri

A thesaurus, in the lexicographical sense, is a classification of words and phrases of similar meaning intended to help writers find the word or words with the exact shade of meaning they want for a particular composition. The best-known example (it is not the only one) is P.M. Roget's *Thesaurus*, first published in 1852 and now available in several rival updated editions. The one recommended for examination is the latest revision from Roget's original publisher, *Roget's thesaurus of English words and phrases* revised by Susan M. Lloyd (Longman, 1982).

Dictionaries of American English

A brief word is necessary on dictionaries of American English. Although for more than a century Americans have insisted they have their own language and their own literature (Matthew Arnold refused to admit it), the leading British and American dictionaries of English are freely available on both sides of the Atlantic. Noah Webster, a pioneer American lexicographer of the early nineteenth century, has given his name to a series of dictionaries of English published by the firm of Merriam. Two well-known Merriam—Webster dictionaries are *Webster's new collegiate dictionary*, a good 'campus' dictionary, and *Webster's third new international dictionary of the English language* (Springfield, Mass.: Merriam, 1959, two volumes; *Supplement* 1976) which defines half a million words. This third edition dropped proper names and included colloquialisms, which annoyed some of its loyal users, but apart from its rather small print it remains a very good dictionary which deserves to be available in every British library.

The choice of English dictionaries

English is spoken by about 300 million people as a mother tongue. It is spoken by many millions more as a second language. Not surprisingly, therefore, English dictionaries abound and some guidance in choice handier than the general bibliographies of reference materials is desirable. It is to be found in *Dictionaries: the good book guide special survey* (Braithwaite and Taylor, 1981), an excellent pamphlet, available free to subscribers to the *Good book guide*, on sale to others. It provides not only sensible hints on how to assess a dictionary, but a neat chart comparing the salient features of thirty-five English dictionaries currently available.

Foreign language dictionaries

These include monolingual, bilingual and multilingual (polyglot) dictionaries. The term lexicon also belongs here. Originally this was synonymous with dictionary, but nowadays it is applied only to the dictionaries of ancient languages. Gerald Long has suggested that bilingual dictionaries are used too much:

> Bilingual dictionaries are obviously useful in learning a language, and in translating. But I would have thought the learner's interest was to move on as rapidly as possible to a dictionary in the language of his study. If a translator uses a bilingual dictionary much, it seems to suggest an inadequate grasp of the foreign language, or of his own, or both.[1]

This is an interesting viewpoint, but not a general one. *Walford* is a sound guide to translating dictionaries. A very good example is *Harrap's new standard French and English dictionary*, Part 1: *French–English* (Harrap, 1972), Part 2: *English–French* (1980). As mentioned earlier, some of the translating dictionaries of minor languages published in their native countries are of poor quality. But as Dr Samuel Johnson said: 'Dictionaries are like watches: the worst is better than none, and the best cannot be expected to go quite true'.

A matter of consequence when judging all reference works is the standard of production. This concerns portability, durability, and, above all, legibility. All these are very important when choosing dictionaries.

Further reading

J.R. Hulbert, *Dictionaries: British and American* (2nd edn, Deutsch, 1968), although no longer up to date with its examples, is still worth looking at for its section 'Making a dictionary' and 'The choice of a dictionary'. The author was an eminent American lexicographer.

Higgens, chapter 3, 'Dictionaries' by Kenneth G. Whittaker achieves a nice balance between examples and general observations.

References

1 Long, Gerald, 'Fish fanciers had better stick to Harrap', *Listener, 105* (2706), 2 April 1981, p.434.

9   Monographs

In most libraries the greater part of the non-fiction stock still consists of books and most of these are non-reference books. For convenience these will be called monographs, although most dictionaries regard 'monograph' as being synonymous with 'treatise'. On the other hand, both words are accepted as meaning 'a systematic composition'. For the purposes of reference, study and research it is an advantage that a book should be systematic. But obviously not all non-fiction books are. Some are deliberately miscellaneous in scope (see chapter 15). Others just happen to be so.

The difficulty with monographs is not merely their number, but their wide variations in value and their all too frequent lack of efficient indexes, so that useful information may only be discovered by accident, or zealous searching. Every librarian concerned with an information service should read the *Indexer*, the half-yearly journal of the Society of Indexers and allied societies. It finds some book indexes to praise, but many more to condemn.[1]

Monographs, like reference works, often include information one would not expect to find in them, only it is likely to be less apparent. This information could be brought to light in bibliographies, but often it never is. Library classification can sometimes be of help. It is likely that at least some of the books brought together on the shelves of a library under the heading 'Histories of London' will include something on the Crystal Palace, the subject of an enquiry, but useful information in biographies of Prince Albert and Sir Joseph Paxton and two valuable chapters in K.W. Luckhurst, *The story of exhibitions* (Studio, 1951) may not so readily declare themselves.

We have heard a good deal about the scattering of information in periodicals, as a considerable amount of money and effort has been spent on bringing periodical information under control. But although bibliographies of monographs also abound, they are seldom analytical. It is a well-known fact that research workers, especially in the humanities, like to browse in libraries and feel very frustrated if they are denied access to library stacks. Donald J. Urquhart, first librarian of what is now called the British Library Lending Division, doubts whether this is necessary. In the course of a discussion on the 'self renewing' proposal for university libraries Dr Urquhart said:

> Undoubtedly three centuries ago browsing was necessary, because there were no bibliographies and it was practicable because of the small volume of publications. But the situation has changed. Nowadays bibliographies exist in most subject fields. . . . If the bibliographies are inadequate then the first necessary step is to improve them; for surely the research worker is or should be interested in what exists on a particular topic rather than what a particular library contains on that topic (or, worse still, what he happens to stumble across in browsing round the shelves). It is not clear to what extent browsing results from the absence of suitable bibliographies, or ignorance about bibliographies, or intellectual laziness.[2]

As a researcher with a wider knowledge of bibliographies than most, I can certify that bibliographies in the humanities, at least, are often non-existent or defective. Where they do exist they often do not go back many years and there is little hope of filling the gaps. I have never been able to rely absolutely on bibliographies in any piece of research I have done. (The subjects include not only librarianship but local history, theatrical history, industrial archaeology and English literature during the 1890s.) Whatever Dr Urquhart may say, the day will probably never come when browsing will be unnecessary. The main difficulty is that the compilation of analytical bibliographies can be very expensive and money to support bibliographical work is far easier to obtain for 'practical' subjects than for history, art, literature and so on.

Fortunately, the increase over the past few decades in the number of special libraries, special departments, and special collections, and the flair librarians develop with experience in finding information concealed in monographs, are of great help to research scholars in their work.

When searching for information in monographs one can sometimes be hindered by non-descriptive titles, although when a book is in the stock of a closely classified library this problem is lessened. The use of non-descriptive titles is very common in the field of biography, but it is to be found everywhere, even among government publications. The report of a government committee on sewage disposal was called

Clean and decent. Bruce Catton's story of the Union side of the American Civil War is called *This hallowed ground*.

References

1   Bakewell, K.G.B., 'Why are there so many bad indexes?', *Library Association Record, 81* (7), July 1979, pp. 330–1.
2   Urquhart, D.J., 'University libraries: the case for a national lending system', *Times Higher Educational Supplement, 256*, 17 September 1976, p.8.

10 Encyclopedias

Dictionaries tell us that 'encyclopedia' derives from a Greek word meaning 'a complete circle of learning'. The *purpose* of an encyclopedia is not discussed in dictionaries. According to Frances Neel Cheney its function is 'to synthesize existing knowledge in a form that can be retrieved easily'.[1] The term is used rather loosely, but this applies to most terms concerning reference sources. It is usually applied to the great mutli-volume encyclopedias (with the well-known exception of *Grove's dictionary of music and musicians*) but small-scale encyclopedias, especially the one-volume subject encyclopedias, are published under a variety of names, among them the ingenious term 'companion', used with great success by Oxford University Press for the past fifty years.

There is a substantial literature on encyclopedias, general and subject, but most of it is unknown to encyclopedia users, and even to librarians, although it would seem that American librarians are more conscientious than British in this respect, as they need to be, as no other country produces so many encyclopedias. Because of their high cost, which can be as much as £1,000, large-scale encyclopedias cannot be purchased idly. Constance Winchell recommended that they should be seen before purchase, which is good advice if it can be acted upon.

A comprehensive survey of individual encyclopedias will not be attempted here. But a few examples which merit examination will serve to indicate the characteristics of encyclopedias, which are expensive to produce and easy to fault.

Large-scale encyclopedias: general

The inevitable starting point when reviewing the large-scale general encyclopedias is the *Encyclopædia Britannica*, the one most libraries have and the one most library users have heard of. The *Britannica* is a particularly good starting point because its history shows how difficult it is for even a resourceful and experienced encyclopedia publisher to overcome all the problems encyclopedias are heirs to.

The *Britannica* was first published in Edinburgh, 1768–71. It soon became a national institution, but by the 1920s it had become so costly to produce that no British publisher was prepared to take it over. It was therefore sold to an American firm and has been published in the USA ever since. But as there is a London office, and many of the contributors are British, it could be regarded as an Anglo-American encyclopedia, but probably few librarians regard it so. When it was a British publication it was given cover-to-cover revision at rather long intervals, during which there might be supplementary volumes. American policy has always been to update the *Britannica* annually, a process called 'continuous revision', a practice now used by the publishers of several other American general encyclopedias. Also, strenuous attempts have been made to sell the *Britannica* to private purchasers by accenting its value as a self-educator. There is a good reason for this. Without sales to private purchasers a large-scale general encyclopedia cannot exist. Library sales are not enough.

The traditional provision in the *Britannica* of long, authoritative articles on the major aspects of knowledge meant that, in theory, it could be used for study, but even the provision of an elaborate index volume did not make it a handy source for quick reference. For this reason, and probably also because an American scholar, Harvey Einbinder, had published a detailed criticism of the *Britannica*, in a book called *The myth of the Britannica*, for its fifteenth (1974) edition the publishers adopted an entirely new pattern.[2] The *Britannica* is now, in effect, two encyclopedias in one. The 'Macropaedia' consists of long articles suitable for continuous reading and for study, and the 'Micropaedia' consists of short articles for quick reference. The two parts are linked by cross-references. There is also a third part, a one-volume 'Propaedia', a schematic study guide to the encyclopedia. This is interesting, as it indicates the structure of the encyclopedia, but most users ignore it. Although this radical change in the organisation of the information in the *Britannica* had a mixed reception, it is a praiseworthy attempt to overcome a basic difficulty with large-scale encyclopedias intended primarily for home use.

There remains the problem of keeping the *Britannica* up to date. Continuous revision is only a partial solution. For one thing it is not possible to up-date the whole encyclopedia every year. For another, it is not possible for purchasers, even libraries, to buy the *Britannica* every year. There is a *Britannica year book*, an excellent reference work in its own right, but reading a basic article in the encyclopedia, and then following it through several issues of the *Year book*, is more than most people are prepared to do.

One of Harvey Einbinder's major complaints about the *Britannica*, when he surveyed it in 1964, before it had been completely overhauled, was that some of the major articles, especially in the humanities, had not been revised for many years. It must be admitted that the average user of an encyclopedia can more readily detect out-of-date articles on matters such as television, civil aviation, space travel, and the local and national government of Britain in the 1980s, than articles about the archaeology of Roman Britain, the interpretation of Shakespeare's sonnets, the private life of James Boswell, and appreciations of the compositions of Schubert and Mozart which do not refer to the recent discoveries of forgotten manuscripts. On the other hand, some of the major articles contributed to large-scale general encyclopedias were written by authors of the greatest eminence and for that reason are still worth looking at. Unfortunately, too few of the articles contributed to general encyclopedias by famous writers and academics have been reprinted in book form. Among the exceptions are the biographical articles of Macaulay and the studies in musicology by Sir Donald Tovey, all of which were contributed to the *Encyclopædia Britannica*.

A careful examination of the most recent reprint of the latest edition of the *Encyclopædia Britannica*, and a brief study of its history, will provide a useful knowledge of the peculiarities of major general encyclopedias which will be of great help when examining other large-scale encyclopedias. A cynic has said that the use of these reference works by the intelligent and well-informed is the triumph of hope over experience. Librarians engaged upon queries are likely to go to more specialised and more recent sources of information, but they should not despise those of their readers who turn to encyclopedias more frequently. They should be used with discretion, but by and large they are typical of all reference works available in libraries: they include a wealth of potentially useful information which is never used.

Several notable large-scale general encyclopedias are published in the USA, apart from the *Britannica*. Among those worth stocking in British libraries are the *Encyclopedia*

Americana, a splendid encyclopedia particularly useful for its coverage of American topics. There is much to be said also for *Colliers encyclopedia*, which has been carefully edited so that its articles are within the comprehension of teenage readers. A grave fault in a general encyclopedia is the publication of articles by experts which can only be understood by experts.

There is now no large-scale British general encyclopedia. *Everyman's encyclopædia* (6th edn, Dent, 1978, 12 vols) is a good medium-sized work of established reputation, but it would be better with colour illustrations and an analytical index. Although it is aimed at younger readers, the *New Caxton encyclopædia* (5th edn, Caxton Publishing Co., 1979, 20 vols) is worth providing in an adult library by virtue of its admirably clear text and helpful illustrations.

Before taking leave of large-scale encyclopedias there are two more points to be considered. One is the provision in libraries of foreign language encyclopedias. There are several good ones, especially in French and German. Apart from anything else, they have a useful slant towards the geographical, historical and other aspects of their own countries. But the unfortunate fact is that British readers, even in universities, are reluctant to use foreign language works, with the marginal exception of the *Petit Larousse illustré*.

The second point is that a large-scale encyclopedia which was well esteemed in its day will be useful in the future to historians, not merely for its facts, but for its ethical and social attitudes. An illuminating subject to investigate in old general encyclopedias is 'Negroes'.

Large-scale encyclopedias: subject

The number and variety of large-scale subject encyclopedias has increased considerably since World War II. The standard is usually high, as it has to be in subjects such as science, technology, medicine and the law. A few special encyclopedias are produced by professionals for professionals — a good example is the *British encyclopædia of medical practice* — but most of .them are written by experts for general use. Once again one turns to the USA for popular examples, such as the *McGraw Hill encyclopedia of science and technology* (5th edn, New York: McGraw Hill, 1982, 15 vols). This is described in *Higgens* as 'covering the whole field of science and technology', which broadly speaking it does, although it does not include biographical and historical articles. An excellent example in another major field of knowledge is *The international encyclopedia of the social sciences* (New York: Macmillan and The Free Press, 1968). This has a *Biographical supplement*, a feature worth copying.

There is one large-scale British special encyclopedia which is a classic of the genre. I refer to *The new Grove dictionary of music and musicians* (Macmillan, 1980, 20 vols). This is the latest edition of a reference work first published a century ago under the editorship of Sir George Grove.

As the sale of large-scale general encyclopedias is mainly to libraries, the demand for them is not enough to allow for frequent revision. Annual or occasional supplements are therefore common.

Surprisingly, there is a large-scale encyclopedia on librarianship, namely, the *Encyclopedia of library and information science* (New York: Dekker, 1968–82, 33 vols; *Supplement*, 1984). Unfortunately, this is an example (a rare one among large-scale encyclopedias) of a badly planned encyclopedia. Its publication was spread over too many years and it was not compiled according to a rational scheme. A third disability, which could still be put right, is the lack of a comprehensive index.

Small-scale encyclopedias: general

The production of a one-volume general encyclopedia is a challenge in itself. It has been met successfully by two British publishers with *The new Hutchinson twentieth century encyclopædia* (first published by Hutchinson in 1948 and frequently revised) and the newer *Macmillan encyclopedia* (Macmillan, 1981). In both the accent is on geographical and biographical information, but everything is presented clearly and succinctly so that these encyclopedias belong more to desks than library shelves.

Small-scale encyclopedias: subject

Small-scale subject encyclopedias, often called 'dictionaries', are numerous and many good ones are available in paperback. In a handy-size single volume it is possible for an author to compile a subject encyclopedia single-handed.

This has been done several times for the popular 'companions' published by the Oxford University Press, and with great success by Leslie Halliwell in *Halliwell's filmgoer's companion* (7th edn, Granada Publishing, 1980). But teams of experts are also often used, as in the *Dictionary of world history* (Nelson, 1973) and the *Cambridge encyclopedia of Russia and the Soviet Union* (Cambridge University Press, 1982), described by one reviewer as 'a beautifully packaged volume of information'. In this encyclopedia, however, the information is not presented under alphabetical headings. Not all works called encyclopedias are arranged alphabetically.

The boundaries between small-scale subject encyclopedias and 'data books' and 'year books' are not always clear. *Kempe's engineer's year book*, for example, is encyclopedic.

Further reading

Higgens, chapter 4 'General encyclopædias' by A.J. Walford and chapter 5 'Subject encyclopædias' by Denis J. Grogan include descriptions of a fair number of titles, but they also give the reader a good idea of how to assess an encyclopedia. William A. Katz, *Introduction to reference work*, vol. 1, *Basic information sources* (4th edn, McGraw Hill, 1982) chapter 6 'Encyclopædias: general and subject' is very good on American large-scale encyclopedias. See also Harvey Einbinder 'Encyclopædias: some foreign and domestic developments', *Wilson Library Bulletin, 55* (4), December 1980, pp.257—61.

A good deal can be learnt about the virtues and defects of large-scale encyclopedias by reading the following meticulous reviews of two of them: C.D. Needham 'Britannica revisited', *Library Association Record 77* (7), July 1975, pp.153—68 and E.V. Corbett 'Encyclopedia of library and information science', *Journal of Librarianship, 9* (2), April 1977, pp. 148—55. This review was written when only volumes 1 to 18 had been published, but Corbett's general criticisms still apply.

References

1 Cheney, Frances Neel, 'Encyclopedias' in *ELIS*, vol. 8 (1972) pp.45—8.
2 Einbinder, Harvey, *The Myth of the Britannica*, (MacGibbon & Kee, 1964).

11   Yearbooks

The term 'yearbook' is used by publishers for a variety of reference works published annually, and even for some which are not. Some of these publications would be better called directories. The term will be used here to cover two types of annual publication, namely, digests of current information on the UK and other countries and annual reviews of world history.

With regard to the first group there are, of course, two well-known reference works which have a place in the stock of many libraries. It should not be supposed, however, that every librarian is fully aware of what may be found in *Whitaker's almanack* and the *Statesman's year book*. This is certainly not true. One comes to the rueful admission that librarianship is a profession with too many tools.

This chapter overlaps others. This cannot be helped. Until we can put all our faith in computers we must cope with the idiosyncracies of packages of information as they happen to be produced in printed form. The more popular yearbooks will now be considered individually.

Whitaker's almanack, 1868 (Whitaker, published annually). The variety of information in *Whitaker* is more than most people realise. A reviewer of the 1981 edition said 'One imagines that if half the world were destroyed by atomic war, Whitaker's would still be available in the best fall-out shelters, reciting the latest changes in the consular representation of Swaziland and the stipend of the Bishop of Sodor and Man'. Two things worth remembering about *Whitaker* are (a) its accent on current information about the UK, and (b) a good deal of this information relates to senior office holders (political, administrative, ecclesiastical, academic and so on). Inevitably, some of this information becomes outdated as the year progresses. A general election, for example, is very unkind to *Whitaker*. Note the spelling of *Almanack* (like *Britannica*, a trap for the negligent) and also that the index to *Whitaker*, a good one, is at the front of the volume, a sensible feature which other yearbooks should copy.

Statesman's year book, 1854 (Macmillan, published annually). This is an authoritative digest of information on individual countries preceded by a section on the international organisations. It is appropriately sub-titled 'Statistical and historical annual of the states of the world'. The concealed bibliographies are not as helpful as they could be, but this is a common failing in reference works.

Europa year book: a world survey, 1959 (Europa, published annually, two volumes). Like the *Statesman's year book*, this work has an unhelpful title. As its sub-title indicates, it covers not only Europe but the world. But it is more informative than the *Statesman's year book* as it includes detailed information such as lists of office holders and statistical tables and directory information such as lists of banks.

The standard year book on the UK is one of the better-known British government publications: Central Office of Information, *Britain: an official handbook*, 1946 — HMSO, published annually. Drawing largely on official sources of information (poorly acknowledged in the bibliography) this is a sound work to read or refer to on the major aspects of the British way of life — government, trade, industry, education, religion and so forth.

There are several yearbooks, mostly published in association with well-known American encyclopedias, which keep track of recent events in systematic annual reviews. Two good examples are *Annual register*, 1761 (Longman, published annually) and the *Britannica book of the year*, 1938 (Chicago: Encyclopædia Britannica). The former is a review of political, economic and cultural events at home and abroad and has been published continuously since the age of Edmund Burke, who was its first editor. Its value is cumulative. To researchers in modern history a complete set is a boon. It is now compiled by 100 expert contributors. Although the greater part of the latter is an alphabetical sequence of short articles designed for quick reference, thus, in effect, up-dating the *Britannica*, there is a section of long feature articles.

Further reading

Higgens, chapter 8 'Newspapers and other material on recent events' by Geoffrey Whatmore.

12 Newspapers

Newspapers originated in the seventeenth century as newsletters and news sheets. They achieved daily publication, with a fair coverage of news and advertisements, in the eighteenth century. Unfortunately, their development and circulation were gravely hampered for many years in Britain by government taxes such as the stamp tax. The last of these was not removed until 1861. Thereafter, progress was rapid. By the end of the nineteenth century there were national newspapers to suit all sections of the community and in many towns there were rival local newspapers. In recent years a number of old established local newspapers have had to cease publication, but free ones, with the accent on advertisements, have taken their place. Although librarians have little regard for these free newspapers, they should not neglect to preserve them.

Newspapers are used increasingly in libraries for historical as well as current information. For whatever purpose they are required they generate problems which cannot always be overcome. Libraries have requests for files of newspapers published before they themselves were established. The files they have got will occupy an extravagant amount of space. Worse still, newspapers published during the past hundred years or so, because they were printed on inferior paper, made from mechanical wood pulp, will have become brittle. (By contrast, the earliest newspapers, printed on rag paper, are likely to be in remarkably good condition.) Fortunately, these difficulties have been largely overcome by the use of microfilm. Microfilm copies not only close the gaps in newspaper holdings, but prevent handling of the deteriorating originals. The saving of space is enormous; so is the labour of handling bound volumes.

Following the successful marketing of complete runs of important national newspapers, such as *The Times*, the more exacting task of making complete microfilm sets of hundreds of provincial newspapers has been undertaken, a vital project now assisted by the British Library's Newspaper Library. Despite the difficulty of scanning the large pages of newspapers on small screens, microfilm copies of newspapers have been very welcome, especially when they are consulted in reading machines with print-out facilities, although the quality of the prints is often far from ideal.

The problem to which there is no easy solution is the general lack of complete newspaper indexes. The most notable exceptions are the published indexes to *The Times* and the *New York Times*. But although for the greater part of the present century the index to *The Times* is fairly good, for the whole of the nineteenth century, and a few years before and after, it is unsatisfactory. This is because for the period 1790 to 1905 we have only the unofficial and highly selective *Palmer's Index to The Times*. Since 1906 there has been a much superior index published either by *The Times* itself, or by one of its subsidiaries, now called Research Publications. Since 1973, this official index has also covered *The Sunday Times* and since 1977 it has been published monthly with annual cumulations, thus giving *The Times* the best pattern of indexing it has ever had. Research Publications have recently given us indexes for the period 1785–9, hitherto lacking.

Even in its present form *The Times Index* is not ideal. This becomes evident when one compares it with the superb *New York Times Index*, 1851 to date, which not only indexes the news but abstracts it. It is also online.

It is appropriate to mention here *Keesing's Contemporary Archives* (Longman Group), an impartial digest of world news published now in monthly loose-leaf instalments (until 1982 they were weekly) with interim and final name and 'analytical' (country and topical) indexes for each year. *Keesing's* began publication in 1932. All the back volumes have recently been published on microfiche. Although *Keesing's* cites the names of leading newspapers among its declared sources of information, unfortunately it does not give specific references to them. The American equivalent to *Keesing's* is called *Facts on file*.

Most public libraries, either through lack of staff, or lack of foresight, did not begin to index their files of local newspapers until the present century, and in some cases well into it. (One city library, which opened its doors in 1883, did not start indexing the local press until 1934. This is probably an average example.) In a few public libraries, among them Nottingham and Dumfries, work is now underway on the unindexed volumes, but retrospective indexing is a fearsome task and without voluntary help difficult to accomplish.

Indexing is important, but by itself it is not enough. For

example, a researcher working on say, the history of a town's cinemas (a likely subject now that most cinemas have disappeared) is not likely to be altogether grateful for 167 references scattered through 68 bound volumes and 53 spools of microfilm. The major news items, at least, should be available also in a classified collection of mounted newscuttings. These will not only aid research but facilitate photocopying.

As one would expect, the exploitation of newspapers as sources of information has reached a high standard in the libraries of our national newspapers and broadcasting organisations. (See the manual by Geoffrey Whatmore cited below.) Local libraries, on the whole, have less urgent demands for news information. Certainly they have less generous labour and other resources to cope with them. The following observation by a local historian who had been working on the history of Leicestershire windmills points to the difficulties encountered all too often by local historians: 'A careful search of 18th and 19th century local newspapers (a job for a team rather than an individual) would undoubtedly reveal a good deal of information . . .'.[1]

Fortunately, the British Library's great Newspaper Library at Colindale, which has twenty miles of shelving for its extensive files of national and local newspapers, is not only dealing zealously with its own problems, but is helping other libraries with theirs, not only by microfilming files of local newspapers, but by publishing an informative *Newsletter* (see below) on what is being done around the country in the cause of newspaper acquisition, preservation and exploitation.

Some years ago, the Reference, Special and Information Section of the Library Association began work on a comprehensive *Bibliography of British newspapers*, listing, with locations, local British newspapers, county by county. This worthy project has now been taken over by the British Library. The first two volumes, *Durham and Northumberland* and *Kent*, were published in 1982.

Further reading

The leading authority on newspapers as sources of information is Geoffrey Whatmore, who had extensive experience, first as librarian of *The Guardian* and latterly as head of the BBC News Library. He wrote *Higgens*, chapter 8 'Newspapers and other material on recent events', but it is worthwhile looking also at his book *The modern news library* (Library Association, 1977).

On the history and present-day production of *The Times Index* see Barbara James 'Indexing *The Times*', *The Indexer, 11* (4), October 1979, pp.209–11.

The *British Library Newspaper Library newsletter*, mentioned above, is published half-yearly and distributed free of charge by the British Library Newspaper Library, Colindale Avenue, London NW9 5HE. On the Newspaper Library itself see Alan Day, 'A Colindale reverie', *New Library World, 80* (954), December 1979, pp.238–40.

On newspapers as sources of local history see Harold Nichols, *Local studies librarianship* (Bingley, 1979) pp. 84–7 and the *Local Studies Librarian*, the half-yearly journal of the Local Studies Group of the Library Association, especially volume 1 (2), Summer 1982, which is largely devoted to this topic.

On the history of newspapers see the article 'Newspaper' in *Chambers encyclopedia*, volume 9 (Pergamon Press, 1967).

References

1   Bennett, J.D., 'Windmills in Leicestershire', *Leicestershire Historian*, Spring 1971, p.25.

13 Periodicals

Once again we are up against the problem of definition. Many librarians regard 'periodical' as synonymous with 'serial', particularly in the USA, where the term serial is preferred. (Strangely, there is no entry in *ELIS* under either term.) In Britain, usage varies, but serials is often regarded as an omnibus term for all publications which appear serially, not only periodicals and newspapers, but annual reports, yearbooks, directories and so forth. In this chapter we are concerned only with the nature and value of periodicals. The bibliographic control of them, and the even more difficult task of exerting bibliographical control over the contributions to periodicals, are dealt with respectively in chapters 29 and 30. A periodical is taken to be a publication intended to appear at intervals, regular or irregular, for an indefinite period, and usually having several features by different contributors.

Certain types of periodicals have their own terms, for example 'house journals' and 'little magazines'. A *house journal* is a company periodical produced for the staff, the customers, or potential customers. House journals are quite numerous. At their best, they are of great value. A *little magazine* is a shoestring journal which gives budding literary authors a chance to appear in print. It is likely to be the organ of an *avant-garde* group and more kindly disposed towards new poets than the major literary journals. Several modern authors who are now well-known were glad to appear in little magazines in their youth. Ironically, files of the original issues of little magazines published in the early decades of this century, when they could have been acquired for a few shillings, or a few cents a copy, are now being purchased by research libraries, even in facsimile reprints, at high prices.

Periodicals as a whole can be divided into two broad groups. The smaller is *primary periodicals*. These are concerned wholly, or mainly, with the results of original research. They may be of small circulation, but will be of high quality, the articles in them having been carefully vetted. The other and larger group is *secondary periodicals*. These often have originality in content and treatment, but their main purpose is not to extend the boundaries of our knowledge of the arts and sciences. These extensions can often be of very limited interest anway.

The history of periodicals

Periodicals began tentatively in the seventeenth century. They became familiar publications among the educated and tolerably affluent in the mid-eighteenth century, the age of Johnson. A famous example born in that period was the *Gentleman's Magazine* (1731–1907). Although the nineteenth century was rich in periodicals, their development was hindered until the 1860s by government taxes. The present century has seen the decline of family magazines (for example, *The Strand*) and weekly reviews (for example, *Saturday Review*), which prospered in the nineteenth century and in the early years of this century, but all other kinds of periodicals have increased in number, especially the non-commercial periodicals published by societies and institutions. No one knows how many periodicals are published today. Although the laws of legal deposit demand periodicals, they do not net all of them. Many of the non-commercial periodicals are produced for private circulation and without the aid of a printer. A public library which knows all the periodicals produced in its own area will be uncommonly well informed.

Problems with periodicals

Periodicals have given rise to many problems in libraries. Throughout the present century considerable efforts have been made to overcome them, within the library profession and still more outside it. A substantial monograph could be written on the effect of periodicals on modern library practice. It was because of the deluge of periodical information and the difficulty of finding it, obtaining it and exploiting it that libraries created special schemes of co-operation among themselves, such as the pioneer regional scheme now called SINTO (Sheffield Interchange Organisation), and compiled location lists (union catalogues) of periodicals, national and local, culminating in the massive *British union catalogue of periodicals (BUCOP)*, rented or purchased photocopying machines, acquired microforms and microform readers, and installed online computer terminals. It should be remembered, also, that it was the gross deficiencies in the provision of periodical information, especially in science and technology, which led the British government to establish the National Lending Library of Science and Technology, now the British Library Lending Division, in 1962.

Outside the library profession considerable capital and ingenuity have been invested in the compilation, originally for publication, of serial indexing and abstracting services, and more recently the transfer of this bibliographical information to computerised databases which are now accessible to subscribers in lieu of, or in addition to, the printed versions. It seems probable that, before long, we shall have the additional benefits of the facsimile transmission of pages from periodicals, and electronic journals which have no counterpart in printed form. We should already be grateful, although some of our readers may not be; for the reissue in microfilm of back files of periodicals whose originals are unobtainable.

A problem with regard to periodicals too obvious to call for comment is the cost of purchasing them and housing them. Books are now expensive, but periodicals are more so as their cost is recurring. Where periodicals have to be acquired by a library in large numbers to support advanced study and research, a large part of the book fund will be automatically bespoken. A university library is likely to have 5,000 periodicals even when it is newly founded. No library can be self-sufficient in periodicals, however. The BLLD and local co-operative schemes can be of help in this matter, but problems remain. One is the deterioration of the postal service. Another is the problem of copyright in so far as it concerns photocopying. It is a problem which does not cease to exist because it is ignored.

The value of old periodicals

When asked why periodicals are important, student librarians are likely to say 'Because they provide up-to-date information'. This is broadly true, although it should be appreciated that the more learned periodicals are apt to keep authors waiting for as much as two years before publishing their 'new' ideas or information. More important to remember is that the back issues of periodicals are valuable because they are an almost inexhaustible quarry of information on the world and beliefs of our predecessors. The main facts have been siphoned off by the authors of monographs and compilers of reference works. We do not have to indulge in protracted periodical research to discover the main facts about Gladstone's political life. But periodical research will throw some light on public reaction to his policies and achievements when in office.

At this point we come to the incidence of use of files of periodicals. In science and technology it is different from that in the humanities, where there is more interest in the past. A good illustration of this is the considerable and growing use of Victorian periodicals by researchers in history and literature in Britain and the USA. The reasons for this interest have been expressed by John S. North as follows:

> The Victorian age is the first for which we have as sensitive a record of a civilisation as the periodical press . . . . Periodical literature is the largest single source of Victorian material available to us and the most comprehensive.

These observations have been extracted from the first chapter of an excellent symposium which is more readable than its title may suggest: *Victorian periodicals: a guide to research* edited by J. Don Vann and Rosemary T. Van Arsdel (New York: Modern Language Association of America, 1978).

In 1969, a Research Society for Victorian Periodicals (RSVP) was founded in the USA. It has since extended its interests to the periodicals of the early nineteenth century and the Edwardian period. There is a British branch. The RSVP's quarterly periodical, the *Victorian Periodicals Review* (University of Toronto for the Society) indicates admirably the Society's interests and the variety of work being done by its members on the history, bibliography and the location of surviving files of nineteenth century periodicals.

A peculiarity of Victorian periodicals is that most of the contributions to them were published anonymously, or pseudonymously, a major handicap to researchers. Fortunately, by examining publishers' archives and authors' correspondence it is possible to identify many of the unsigned contributions. This exacting work was begun some years ago in the USA and the results are being published, periodical by periodical, in the *Wellesley index to Victorian periodicals 1824–1900* (three vols., University of Toronto Press/Routledge & Kegan Paul, 1966–79; in progress). The late Walter E. Houghton, first editor of this unusual kind of bibliography, has said 'The importance of Victorian periodicals to modern scholars can scarcely be appreciated'.

New formats

The great majority of periodicals published today are traditional in form. In literary form they are miscellanies; in physical form they are printed documents. For various reasons — to reduce the cost of printing and distribution, as well as delays in publication, and to isolate individual articles — other ways of publishing periodicals, or the writings submitted to them, have been suggested. In 1948, Professor J.D. Bernal argued that scientific papers should not appear in periodicals, but as separate pamphlets published by a small number of distribution centres. (Many scientific papers were then, as many still are, distributed separately as preprints, offprints and research reports.)

A few periodicals of limited appeal have been published solely in microfiche. At present research is in progress at the universities of Birmingham and Loughborough to find an acceptable way of producing electronic journals. In the meantime the number of printed periodicals increases day by day. The term 'printed' is used in its widest sense, as quite a number of periodicals are produced by societies and institutions from their office machinery.

The United Kingdom Serials Group

Interest in periodicals is so widespread that the creation of a forum where publishers, periodical agents and librarians could discuss mutual problems was inevitable. Such an organisation, the United Kingdom Serials Group, was established in 1978. It holds conferences, organises courses and has a developing programme of publications. It already has an informative *Newsletter*.

Further reading

The best textbook to read on periodicals generally, and their handling in libraries, is Donald Davinson, *The periodicals collection* (2nd edn, Deutsch, 1978), see Parts One and

Three. On the role of periodicals in particular types of library (university, public, special and national) see *Serials librarianship* edited by Ross Bourne (Library Association, 1980), Part 2 'Libraries', but read Davinson first.

The value of scientific and technical periodicals in libraries is discussed at length in *Grogan*, chapter 9 'Periodicals'.

On the case for electronic periodicals and the problems of producing them see John Senders 'An on-line scientific journal', *Information Scientist, 11* (1), March 1977, pp.3—9, and B. Shackel and others 'The BLEND-LINC project on electronic journals after two years', *Aslib Proceedings, 35* (2), February 1982, pp.77—91.

On the aims and activities of the United Kingdom Serials Group see David P. Woodworth 'The UK Serials Group', *Aslib Proceedings, 34* (3), March 1982, pp.188—91. The file of the Group's *Newsletter* (at present half-yearly) is worth looking at.

14 Conference proceedings

Conferences abound. They deal with all subjects, but are particularly rife in science and technology, where about 10,000 a year are now held throughout the world. Some conferences, including many (but not all) of those organised by learned societies and professional associations, are held at regular intervals, usually annually, but many are unique, conferences held for special purposes, such as the International Conference on National Bibliographies (Paris, September 1977), sponsored by UNESCO and IFLA.

There is not much to say about conference proceedings in themselves. Like periodicals, collections and Festschriften they are most often discussed by librarians for the bibliographical problems they present, which will be dealt with in chapter 31. Although there is talk now of 'videoconferencing', it seems hardly likely that experience will triumph over hope, and professional men and women will foresake the trouble (they may be relieved of the expense) of travelling anything from three to 3,000 miles to a conference with a promising programme.

Although there is some scepticism about the value of conference papers as sources of information, they are probably no better or worse than the non-conference contributions to periodicals, which may be of seminal importance, or a rehash of information already available. But the value of conference papers, like that of articles expressly written for periodicals, is likely to be diminished through delays in publication.

Further reading

Grogan, chapter 13 'Conference proceedings' is concerned with the proceedings of conferences in science and technology, on which it is a very good source of information.

15 Collections, festschriften and anthologies

The pattern of sources of information on a subject is never neat and tidy, least of all in the traditional printed forms. Periodicals are not the only printed sources which are miscellaneous in topics and contributors. There is a vast number of books which are also varied in content. Some of them are carefully structured works of reference, which have been dealt with in other chapters. Our concern here is with miscellanies designed for reading, if only desultory reading. There are two main types:

(a) collections of original writings, which include Festschriften;
(b) collections of previously published writings, which include anthologies.

Collections of original writings

There are many of these. Most of them are volumes commissioned by commercial publishers, a type too familiar to need comment. A typical example is *Charles Dickens, 1812–1870: a centenary volume*, edited by E.W.F. Tomlin, (Weidenfeld & Nicolson, 1969), in which the life, world and writings of Dickens are discussed in seventeen essays by a number of well-known authors with a knowledge of some particular aspect of Dickens.

Less familiar to the general reading public are the collections of original writings, usually with an academic context, called Festschriften. A Festschrift, more often than not, is a collection of essays in honour of a distinguished scholar who is at, or near, the end of his career, and has reached a significant birthday — sixtieth and seventieth birthdays are favoured anniversaries for this particular honour. But not all personal recipients of Festschriften are academics. There is a trend towards extending the use of the form. The contributors to a Festschrift are likely to include friends and colleagues and, in the case of an academic, former students. The subjects chosen for the essays will reflect the recipient's own interests. A good example is *Larkin at 60*, edited by Anthony Thwaite (Faber, 1982), a volume of essays in honour of Philip Larkin, a distinguished poet who is also an esteemed university librarian. But in one respect this Festschrift is not typical. Because the recipient is widely known and admired, the volume was issued by a commercial publisher and noticed by many reviewers.

The precise origins of Festschriften have never been determined, but they probably originated in Germany, where they have long been numerous. But many have also been produced in the USA. The form is belatedly gaining popularity in Britain.

Miscellanies including original material provide yet another problem for bibliographers which has so far not been satisfactorily dealt with. The most likely way of finding details of the contributions to miscellanies is in the relevant indexing services. For some subjects, including librarianship, there are retrospective analytical bibliographies of Festschriften. There is an American serial bibliography which indexes a number of collections, although it seems to be little used in British libraries: *Essay and general literature index,* 1934–   (New York: H.W. Wilson) half-yearly; annual cumulations.

Collections of previously published writings

In most subjects students are spared a certain amount of tiresome searching for classic writings and official documents of prime importance in their studies because edited collections of them have been published. An outstanding example is the series of volumes published for the use of students of British history under the collective title 'English historical documents' (Eyre & Spottiswoode, 1953–   ) which includes treaties, reports, letters and other texts of prime historical importance. The object of the series is 'to make accessible a wide selection of the fundamental sources of English history'.

There is a good example of collected documents, for practitioners as well as students, in librarianship: *A librarian's handbook* (Library Association, 1977) and *A librarian's handbook,* vol. 2 (1980), both compiled by L.J. Taylor.

Miscellanies of previously published writings also include anthologies. (There are some anthologies of original writings, but the form is most successful when it draws upon writings and authors of established reputation.)

Although this book is primarily concerned with sources of information, anthologies deserve brief mention, if only because they are sometimes used for reference purposes. The standard anthologies are often found in the reference collections of academic and public libraries.

It seems to be a popular belief that anyone can compile an anthology. But few become standard works, and fewer still survive the generation in which they were compiled. The most familiar anthologies are those of poetry and one can usually expect an anthology of poetry compiled by a poet to have some merit. A brilliant example is *Come hither*, compiled by Walter de la Mare (2nd revised edition, Constable, 1928). But the most durable of anthologies of English poetry were compiled by men who wrote a little verse but could hardly be called poets. I refer to *The golden treasury*, compiled by Francis Turner Palgrave (first published in 1861 and in many extended editions since) and the *Oxford book of English verse*, compiled by Sir Arthur Quiller-Couch (Oxford University Press, 1900).

Reference queries on poetry can often be solved with the help of *Granger's index to poetry* (7th edn, New York: Columbia University Press, 1982), which is described in chapter 32.

Not all anthologies are of poetry, of course. They also cover short stories, essays, plays and general prose. But for reasons not hard to find it is difficult to produce an anthology of literary writings other than poetry which is itself a work of art.

Further reading

On Festschriften see the Introduction to *Index to Festschriften in librarianship* compiled by J. Periam Danton (New York: Bowker, 1970).

On anthologies see *ELIS*, volume 1 (1968), 'Anthology and anthologists' by Roy B. Stokes, pp.453–7.

16   Government publications

So far we have dealt with sources of information distinguished by their form. Government publications (hereafter referred to as GPs) are an exception. They have to be considered as a separate group for reasons other than either their physical forms (most of them are still printed publications) or their literary forms (these also are traditional and include monographs, reference works and periodical articles). GPs are not even set apart because of their subjects. The interests of modern governments are so wide that their publications cover almost every subject from accountancy to zoology, with the exceptions of literature and theology. This observation applies not only to the official publications of individual countries, but to those of the great intergovernmental organisations such as the United Nations and its Agencies and the European Communities. GPs are distinguished by their origin, by which is meant their administrative history.

First, however, it should be explained why this chapter is headed 'Government publications' and not 'Official Publications'. The answer is that the term 'official publications' covers not only national but local government publications. (In the USA there are federal, state and local government publications.) But as it is the publications of central governments which cause particular problems for librarians and library users, it seemed better to concentrate on them exclusively.

It is true that some libraries have little or nothing to do with GPs. They are not much in evidence in small public libraries, or in special libraries in the humanities, except libraries concerned with history and archaeology. But in the libraries of universities and polytechnics, in the central libraries of large cities, and in special libraries in pure and applied science, medicine and the social sciences, GPs are an essential part of the stock.

In a university library it usually happens that there is a special collection of GPs, with its own staff. A casual knowledge of GPs and the catalogues of them is not enough when dealing with requests for GPs in a library where they form a large and well-used part of the stock.

GPs in general have certain characteristics, namely:

1 They exist in vast numbers The fact that most of them are pamphlets and leaflets, rather than books, is immaterial. Their importance is not in ratio to their size. Many are serials and many others belong to series, but they still have to be accounted for as individual sources of information. In most countries the government is the largest publisher. But there is a rider to this:

2 A central government publisher will not be the only government publisher Although it is usual for a government to have a central publishing organisation, such as Her Majesty's Stationery Office (HMSO) in the UK, and the United States Government Printing Office in the USA, there is a universal tendency for individual government departments and institutions to act as their own publishers, for at least some of their titles. As a matter of convenience, patent specifications and maps are always published separately, but the drift of other publications away from the centre has created problems of bibliographic control and availability which librarians have found rather tiresome.

3 Most GPs have little publicity Only a small fraction of GPs are individually advertised or reviewed, except perhaps in specialist journals. The exceptions are new laws and reports of investigating commissions and committees on matters of general interest, such as education, social security, and trade unions. This makes scrutiny of the official lists and catalogues essential, the more so because:

4 GPs are selectively covered by the national bibliographies Because of their large number and, with but few exceptions, their limited interest, GPs are included very selectively in the book-trade lists of new publications, if at all. Even the *BNB* is selective in its coverage of British GPs. There is a further bibliographical problem:

5 Official catalogues of GPs are not very informative The ready proof of this is the existence of independent bibliographies of GPs, although these are mainly retrospective. Because it suits the legislature and the civil service, the official catalogues of a country's GPs are commonly arranged by departments and institutions, not by subjects. The catalogue indexes are likely to be unscientific and individual entries will seldom be annotated. The catalogues of the central government publisher are unlikely to record departmental publications published directly. But the catalogues of GPs are one thing; their availability is another.

6 GPs bypass the commercial bookshops Because of

their limited appeal, and the fact that most GPs are still lowly priced, most commercial bookshops take no interest in them. Libraries therefore have to deal direct with the government publishers. They may have to do so anyway to obtain discount or, if there is a repository system, as in the USA, free copies. Any concessions a government may give to libraries with regard to its official publications will be in recognition of the fact that:

7 *GPs can be vital sources of information* Some GPs are merely the dispensable by-products of government offices. But many are important to those to whom they are addressed, who may be members of a particular profession, trade or organisation. This applies not only to current laws but to reports and advisory publications. The latter will deal with matters as various as safety in factories, the teaching of languages in schools and claiming social welfare benefits.

Since World War II there has not only been a considerable increase in the production of GPs but in the demand for them in libraries. Part of this demand has been due to the growth of historical studies, so that old and out of print GPs are now requested as well as those published recently. One interesting result of the increased demand for GPs, new and old, has been the considerable endeavour by independent publishers, bibliographers and experts to make GPs easier to identify and understand and, if they are old, easier to obtain.

What has been said so far about GPs is applicable to all of them, with a few variations. But as the readers of this manual are most likely to be concerned with British GPs, a brief section on their idiosyncracies is necessary.

British government publications

The central government publisher in the UK is HMSO, which has exclusive authority to publish on behalf of Parliament. Parliamentary Publications include statutes, bills, reports on matters of interest to Parliament (note here two important series: Command Papers and House of Commons Papers) and the official reports of the parliamentary debates, commonly known as *Hansard*, in honour of their nineteenth century publisher. Note also the fairly new Parliamentary Publication called the *House of Commons Information Bulletin*, which provides useful information on legislation in progress and House of Commons Committees. This is produced by the House of Commons Public Information Office, which is also responsible for an online information service on Parliament called POLIS.

HMSO also publishes many Non-Parliamentary Publications (including Statutory Instruments, the numerous regulations made under the authority of particular Acts of Parliament), but in recent years many more have been published direct by government departments and institutions, and also by the nationalised industries.

HMSO's serial catalogues are frequent and cumulative. There is a *Daily List* (now accessible via PRESTEL), a *Monthly Catalogue* (its odd official title is *HMSO Books Catalogue*) and an *Annual Catalogue*, to which there is a quinquennial index. HMSO does not publish a complete catalogue of its titles in print. Instead it issues a useful series of departmental and subject *Sectional Lists*.

HMSO operates an elaborate postal service which is augmented, though not widely enough, by sales to personal callers at its own 'Government Bookshops' in London, Birmingham, Bristol, Manchester, Edinburgh, Cardiff and Belfast.

Since 1971 there has been useful liaison between HMSO and the library profession through a Library Association Standing Committee on Official Publications (originally called the HMSO Services Working Party). The activities of this Committee are reported regularly in *Refer*, the half-yearly journal of the Reference, Special and Information Section of the Library Association.

The problem of tracing and obtaining non-HMSO official publications has been largely overcome by the firm of Chadwyck-Healey (Cambridge) which publishes a bi-monthly *Catalogue of British official publications not published by HMSO*, 1980– . The firm can supply most of the titles listed in microfiche.

Most of the British GPs published over the past 200 years have been reprinted by commercial publishers in microform. Many published during the eighteenth and nineteenth centuries have also been reprinted in volume form.

Details of the excellent retrospective bibliographies of British GPs compiled by Professor P. Ford and others need not be given here. But there is one particular unofficial bibliography of British government publications which must be mentioned as it is an essential aid to all who have much to do with these publications. This is Frank Rodgers' *A guide* to *British government publications* (New York: H.W. Wilson, 1980). This unique work is an invaluable source of information on the present-day pattern of British GPs, including their administrative history.

HMSO is the British agent for the publications of various international organisations, including the United Nations and its agencies, but it imports only a selection of them.

A type of information well represented in GPs is statistics. The range and value of these is indicated in chapter 17.

Further reading

On GPs generally see the following articles by a former HMSO official: J.J. Cherns, 'Government publishing: an overview', *IFLA Journal, 4* (4), 1978, pp.351–9, and J.J. Cherns, 'What is the role of government publishers?', *State Librarian, 27* (2), July 1979, pp.16–19.

There is a concise survey of British government publications in *Higgens*, chapter 12 'Government publications' by James G. Ollé. The best introductory textbook is David Butcher, *Official publications in Britain*, (Bingley, 1983). Although this is mainly concerned with British GPs, it also includes a chapter on 'Local government publishing'. An advanced textbook, now in need of revision, is still worth looking at for its chapters on Parliamentary Publications: John E. Pemberton, *British official publications*, (2nd edn, Oxford: Pergamon Press, 1973).

The federal official publications of the USA are far less known in Britain than British GPs are known in the USA. A glance at the *Monthly Catalog of United States Government Publications* will show that there is good reason why official publications are much discussed by the American library profession. Most of the contributors to the bi-monthly *Government Publications Review* (Pergamon Press) are American.

After this chapter had been written the new British government amalgamated the Departments of Trade and Industry. This change in the machinery of government (there have been many since World War II) means a change in the 'authorship' of many British government publications.

17 Statistics

Statistics are numerical facts. They have a long history. Statistics of a kind were recorded in the Domesday Book. But it was not until the late eighteenth century that statistical theory and practice made much progress. In 1801 the British government held its first population census. In 1834 the Royal Statistical Society was founded.

A digest of recent British government statistics published by Penguin Books bears the appropriate title *Facts in focus*. Its Foreword explains why statistics are important:

> Statistics are part of our way of life. Politicians, professional and amateur, argue over them, businessmen and administrators plan with them; trade unionists bargain around them. They are essential to the academic researcher, and every social science student must know where to find a wide range of data.[1]

Statistics are published on a far wider range of topics than most people realise. Fully to appreciate the variety and bulk of present-day statistics one must visit a city library with a commercial department or, better still, the Department of Trade and Industry's Statistics and Market Intelligence Library, 1 Victoria Street, London, a public library too seldom visited by librarians.

Most statistics collected today are collected by governments, as they have need of them for day-to-day administration and long-term planning. Also, only governments have the financial resources and legal sanctions necessary to obtain them. But it must not be forgotten that on some matters there are alternative statistics (sometimes conflicting with the official statistics) from sources such as trade unions, employers' federations and professional associations.

Statistics promulgated by, or under the direction of the organisations that compile them are *primary statistics*. Those published in encyclopedias, yearbooks, textbooks, and so on are not often original, but borrowed and adapted. These are *secondary statistics*. All statistics must be used with caution, but secondary statistics must be used with special caution.

Although government statistics are of major importance, by virtue of their authority and bulk, not all government statistics are published, either because they are 'classified' (that is, confidential) sources of information, or because it is believed that there may be too little interest in them to justify the expense of publication. In the latter case they may be obtainable on request.

Statistics may be misread, with unfortunate results. It is important to take notice of headings and explanatory matter. A common device, to save space, is to abbreviate statistics and print them with a covering note 'These figures represent thousands'. Secondary statistics can sometimes mislead through careless conversion from tables to bar-charts and histograms.

There are three enduring difficulties with regard to statistical information. The first is the poverty of statistics before the nineteenth century. The second is that statistics take time to process, even with the aid of a computer. (The publication of the full range of reports of the decennial population census is a case in point.) The third difficulty is that social statistics are often open to challenge, crime statistics because they are based on detected crimes, tax return statistics because of tax evasion, and unemployment statistics because not everyone out of work bothers to register. Although the criticism of government statistics is a routine exercise for the press and Her Majesty's opposition, it is not always unfair. Unfortunately, only libraries with a sophisticated news service can readily produce commentaries on controversial statistics with the statistics themselves.

The first thing to know about British statistics is that a special government department, the Central Statistical Office (CSO), has the responsibility of collecting statistics from the other government departments and publishing them in convenient form. It does this in a series of digests which should be examined. Note that the sources of these digested statistics are given and that some of them are not government departments but outside bodies, such as the Building Societies Association. The major CSO series of statistical digests are as follows:

Monthly digest of statistics
Annual abstract of statistics
Social trends (annual)
Regional trends (annual)

The *Annual abstract* has a wider range of statistics than the *Monthly digest* and it provides comparative statistics for the previous ten years.

The CSO also provides what it calls 'key economic and social statistics' via PRESTEL. New developments in British government statistics are explained in illustrated articles in the CSO's quarterly journal *Statistical News*. Finally, the CSO is responsible for a comprehensive annotated bibliography of all government and all important non-government statistical publications: *Guide to official statistics* (4th edn, 1982). All the above CSO titles are published by HMSO, which also publishes the detailed statistics compiled by the other government departments which the CSO digests. Among the major producers of statistics are the Office of Population Censuses and Surveys, the Department of Trade and Industry, the Department of Employment and the Department of Education and Science. Almost every government department compiles and publishes a mass of statistics. The *Guide to official statistics* is therefore even more important than the CSO digests in a library which has a good stock of current HMSO publications.

Users of British government statistics and librarians whose particular business is to provide them have been alarmed by the recent threat of cuts in the statistical service. What these could mean will be found in two complementary reports: *Review of government statistical services: report to the Prime Minister by Sir Derek Rayner* (Central Statistical Office, 1980) and *Government statistical services*, Cmnd. 8236 (HMSO, 1981).[2]

For British statistics of the past there is an independent digest which goes back to the twelfth century, although before the eighteenth century there is not much to record: B.R. Mitchell and Phyllis Deane, *Abstract of British historical statistics* (Cambridge University Press, 1962).

For world statistics the handiest authoritative source is the *United Nations statistical yearbook*, 1948– , (New York: United Nations Statistical Office), a well-edited volume which covers a remarkably wide range of statistics. Notice how it deals with data which are not strictly comparable.

Among the secondary sources of statistical information are several well-known yearbooks, for example *Whitaker's almanack*, the *Statesman's yearbook* and the *Municipal year book*. As previously observed, these must be used with care.

Further reading

Higgens, chapter 13 'Statistics as a reference resource' by A. Allott is a good review by a librarian responsible for commercial information in a large city library.

Government statistics: a brief guide to sources is a terse but useful list of the British government's statistical publications. It is revised annually and obtainable free of charge from the Press and Information Service, Central Statistical Office, Great George Street, London SW1P 3AQ.

References

1 Central Statistical Office, *Facts in focus*, (5th edn, Penguin Books, 1980) p.13.
2 See 'The Rayner review of the government statistical service', *Statistical news*, **54**, August 1981, pp.1–4.

18 Directories

Many more directories are published than are to be found in the majority of libraries. To appreciate how many, and how varied they are, one must visit a library of business information (sometimes called a commercial library). There one will find hundreds of directories, British and foreign, general and special. The majority of them most libraries will never need.

We have had directories since the eighteenth century, but the town and county directories which originated then, and were once a familiar part of the stocks of public libraries, have almost disappeared since World War II. (Old copies are to be found in libraries of local studies, as they include a good deal of historical and topographical information.) The decline of the town (street) and county directories has been due, in part, to the vast increase in the number of telephone subscribers, and the publication of classified as well as alphabetical telephone directories.

The obvious defect of directory information in printed form is that it begins to become outdated even while it is going through the press. Some directory information is now available via PRESTEL (tourism addresses notably), but as the sum total of directory information is colossal, it will be a long time before it is available through videotex or online.

Not all directory information is in reference works actually called directories. Some is published in year books, general and special, and personal directory information is also available in a variety of 'who's who' biographical dictionaries.

Libraries in which directories form an important part of the stock will have to face the expense of renewing those published annually and the vexation of making do with those revised infrequently. (It has been calculated that up to 30 per cent of the entries in an annual directory have to be changed.) This is a type of reference work where titles tend to come and go. Several attempts to replace locally Kelly's former street directories have failed. One has to be aware of badly compiled directories produced by unknown, unscrupulous publishers solely to make money out of unwary commercial advertisers.

There is a small number of directories of wide scope and established reputation which many libraries subscribe to and are well worth knowing and these are described in the following paragraphs.

Kelly's post office London directory, (East Grinstead: Kelly's Directories) is published annually. It is not much use for tracing private residents, but is good for commercial and industrial addresses. 'Post Office' in the title simply means that official postal addresses are given. This directory has no official standing.

British Telecom's telephone directories. A complete set of these, which includes the classified directories, is stocked by many libraries. A necessary aid to their use is the *Index to telephone directories*, which tells you which directory covers a particular town or village. Discovering on what principles firms and institutions are listed in both types of telephone directory can be both an amusing and a frustrating experience. Microfiche editions of telephone directories are now becoming available, but their uses will probably be limited.

Kompass register of British industry and commerce, vol. 1: *Products and services*, vol. 2: *Company information* (Haywards Heath: Kompass Publishers) is published annually. The Kompass international series of directories (there are about twenty others) are not only very informative about individual firms, but use an ingenious method of classifying goods and services (see vol. 1) which should be studied.

Kelly's manufacturers and merchants directory (East Grinstead: Kelly's Directories) is published annually. This is a traditional classified and alphabetical directory of British commercial and industrial firms.

A good idea of the number and variety of directories published may be gained by looking at the following bibliographies: *Current British directories* (Beckenham: CBD Research), *Current European directories* (CBD Research) and the *Guide to American directories* (New York: B. Klein Publications). Each of these is frequently revised.

Further reading

This is a topic on which it is advisable to read something

recent but not too wide-ranging. *Higgens*, chapter 7 'Directories and other business publications' by Malcolm J. Campbell is ideal. Browsing in *Walford* is not very helpful, as directories are scattered by subject. A visit to the City Business Library, Gillett House, Basinghall Street, London is recommended.

On the history of British directories and their value in historical research see Jane E. Norton, *Guide to the national and provincial directories of England and Wales, excluding London, Published before 1856*, (Royal Historical Society, 1950) 'Introduction', pp.1–24.

19 Biographical sources of information

There is a demand for biographical information in every library. In some libraries (for example general public reference libraries, newspaper libraries and broadcasting libraries) it accounts for a fair percentage of users' requests.

There are three factors concerning notable persons: time, place and occupation. These are evident if one studies the titles of any good collection of biographical dictionaries. At one extreme there are the universal biographical dictionaries, covering notabilities of all times, countries and occupations. Familiar examples are *Chambers biographical dictionary* (revised edition, W. & R. Chambers, 1974) and *Webster's biographical dictionary* (revised edition, Springfield, Mass: Merriam, 1972). At the other extreme there are dictionaries restricted by two, or even three of the factors mentioned above, such as *Who's who in atoms* (7th edn, Guernsey: Francis Hodgson, 1977), which is international with regard to place, but restricted in time and occupation, and *British authors of the nineteenth century* (New York: H.W. Wilson, 1936), which is restricted in time, place and occupation.

In addition to the information in biographical dictionaries, there is a tremendous amount of biographical information in other reference works, most particularly encyclopedias, where more than one-fifth of the text may be biographical, and yearbooks, which may include 'who's who' sections, or obituaries. Above all, there is the wealth of biographical information buried in the files of newspapers and periodicals.

For many people, not all of them, by any means, famous there are separately published biographies, but these are often unsuitable for providing quick, or even authoritative answers to biographical queries, besides which, even a major research library will have only a selection of biographical monographs.

Biographical queries can not only be difficult, but surprisingly difficult. A good stock of biographical dictionaries is worth having, but they do not, and cannot provide all the answers. Their major defects are:

(a) The exclusion of minor celebrities, people who are known only in their professions, and perhaps not widely in them. (There are many examples in librarianship.)

(b) The absence of people whose fame is recent. (Today, thanks to the media, fame can be very sudden.)

(c) Entries can be out of date. This applies not only to living personalities, but to people of the past, whose recorded life stories need to be corrected, or amplified, in the light of recent research.

(d) An entry which may be very good for one particular query may be inadequate for another.

Two very well-known biographical dictionaries both have serious defects. I refer to the *Dictionary of national biography* (Oxford University Press), commonly known as the *DNB,* and *Who's who* (A & C Black), published annually.

The *DNB* has a peculiar status. No other famous reference work in current use is so much in need of drastic revision or replacement. The original part of it, published by Smith & Elder during the years 1880 to 1905, with a cut-off date about 1900, was a marvellous achievement, and when the work was handed over to the Oxford University Press it must have seemed that its future was assured. But although the OUP have added to it decennial supplements covering notabilities who have died during the present century up to 1970, it has not been able to revise it. There is probably not a single entry which does not need revision. The entries for some celebrities, where modern research has been considerable and revealing (for example, Marlowe, Pepys, Dickens, Marlborough, Queen Victoria) has made the entries for them in the *DNB* grossly imperfect. The bibliographies appended to the entries in the original volumes of the *DNB* tell their own sad story. It is interesting to note that although a great effort was made to include in the *DNB* all those who deserved to be in it, there were a few people whose fame came late, and were therefore excluded, among them Gerard Manley Hopkins, the poet, Sir George Cayley, the pioneer aviator, and Francis Kilvert, the diarist. The great merit of the original volumes is that they were very hospitable to minor celebrities. Unfortunatley, as there is no index of occupations (or of places) it is not easy to identify people who might be interesting to know about. (Some years ago the reference staff of Sheffield Central Library went through the *DNB* and noted all local celebrities, but this probably remains an unusual exercise.)

The twentieth century supplements to the *DNB* do not cast their net as wide as the original volumes. (Librarians have almost disappeared.) Also, it is very difficult to make a fair selection of the recently deceased, and difficult to write about them justly before the appropriate research has been done, and vital private papers released. So the twentieth century *DNB* also invites criticism.

It is very difficult for reference librarians to get to know thoroughly more than a few of the reference works they have to use. That is why, if they can, they cross-check information in more than one source. But the *DNB*'s virtues and defects should be understood. A last point to note (on the credit side) is the handy *Concise DNB*. This is in two volumes. Volume 2 is for the present century and is revised to keep pace with the decennial supplements.

Who's who, a pioneer work of its kind (it was first published in 1849) depends upon information supplied by the subjects in response to a standard questionnaire. One appreciates the defects of this formula when one has to take the chair for a *Who's who* celebrity. One longs for something more akin to a *New Yorker* profile. But note that *Who's who* is not restricted to British personalities, although most entries are British. The volumes of *Who was who*, latterly, like the *DNB*, in decennial volumes, reprint the last entries to appear in *Who's who*, with the addition of dates of death, for notabilities who died during the period 1897 to 1980. The value of these volumes is that they include entries for many people not exalted enough to win a place in the twentieth century *DNB*.

There are many specialised 'who's whos', but the demand for them does not justify annual publication and some fail to survive more than one or two editions. On the other hand, there is a steady increase in the number of specialised retrospective biographical dictionaries. Good examples are the *Dictionary of scientific biography* (New York: Scribners, 1979–80), 14 volumes, an authoritative work of international scope and the *Dictionary of American library biography* (Littleton, Colo.: Libraries Unlimited, 1978).

Biographical queries can be exhausting as well as absorbing. When biographical dictionaries and other reference works fail, scattered sources may have to be tapped. Thanks to the indexing services a fair amount of biographical information in twentieth century periodicals and newspapers can be retrieved. American librarians are fortunate in that they can get the maximum benefit from the *Biography index*

(New York: H.W. Wilson, 1946—), quarterly with annual cumulations. This puts a revealing dragnet through books and periodicals, but it is slanted towards American publications.

The famous *Times* obituaries can be traced in *The Times index*, (see chapter 12), but a *selection* of those published since 1960 have been reprinted in volume form: *Obituaries from The Times 1961—1970* (Reading: Newspaper Archive Developments, 1975) and *1971—1975* (1978).

In a few special libraries where biographical information must be provided, and provided quickly, the staff take pains to augment the reference works and monographs with staff indexes and cuttings files. Not all that is retrieved is accurate in fact, or fair in comment, but these criticisms can be applied to many sources of biographical information in book form.

Sometimes biographical research takes one into the world of genealogy, which may be described as the bare bones of biography. The difficulty here is that one needs a substantial collection of genealogical books and periodicals to make this kind of research profitable.

Further reading

The best thing to read on biographical sources of information is Denis Grogan, *More case studies in reference work* (Bingley, 1972) chapter 3 'Books about people', which consists of case studies of actual biographical queries.

It is worth while grappling with a spool of microfilm to read the anonymous article 'Need to rewrite the DNB', *The Times*, 20 May 1959, p.11.

For newspapers as sources of biographical information see Geoffrey Whatmore, *The modern news library* (Library Association, 1978) chapter 7, 'The personality aspect'.

20   Geographical sources of information

The main types of geographical sources of information are maps and gazetteers. Sometimes they can be found independently; at other times they are complementary.

Maps

Everyone knows what a map is, but the definition of 'map' by R.A. Skelton, formerly Superintendent of the Map Room at the British Museum, is worth quoting: 'A map is a graphic document in which location, extent and direction can be more precisely defined than by the written word; and its construction is a mathematical process strictly controlled by measurement and calculation'.[1]

The provision of maps in libraries has tended to lag behind their publication, and the public's need for them. Even now, there are few separate map libraries, or separate map collections. But the situation is gradually improving.

A knowledge of maps should not begin with the parrot learning of details of major map series, but with an understanding of the elements of cartography, of scales, grids, projections, the representation of relief and the uses of conventional signs. One should know enough about these to visualise a map, a map series, or an atlas from a good description of it.

Maps are now wanted by many people both for work and pleasure. Their use by professional people is considerable. The staffs of central and local government departments need them for a variety of administrative purposes, such as town and country planning. Commercial and industrial firms need them for transport, prospecting and the siting of factories, depots and offices. Students and research workers need maps in many fields, for example, geography, geology, demography, land use, history, archaeology and meteorology. They may have to devise their own maps for their theses and reports.[2]

Many people need maps for workaday or holiday travel, but that is not all. Many have part-time interests which call for the use of maps. Local studies and industrial archaeology (notably with regard to canals and railways) are obvious examples, but the prospectuses of any adult education college will point to others. But although many maps are bought by the public, the need for them in libraries does not lessen; quite the contrary. It is not only an extravagance to buy every map one needs. Not many people know what maps exist, other than the few popular series available in newsagents and bookshops. There is also the important matter of old maps. Many, such as those of William Camden, have been reprinted in facsimile in recent years, but others can only be seen in libraries.

In a library where maps are important, the staff must pay particular attention to them for the following reasons:

(a) Maps communicate information in their own language, which must be understood.

(b) The bibliographic control of maps is still defective, so that an effort must be made to discover what is and has been published. (Atlases are included in the national bibliographies as books, and are therefore easier to keep track of.)

(c) Most maps require special accommodation. Particular care must be taken of rarities.

(d) The existence of maps in a library's stock must be made known by displays and printed publicity.

(e) Attention must be paid to the means by which maps can best be used. It is sometimes possible to lend maps.

It is not unusual for a library's stock of maps to be scattered. In a large city library some may be in the lending library, some in the general reference library, and others in the local studies library. In a university it is likely that some map collections will be held by departments (for example, the geography department) as well as by the university library.

A library must have a fairly precise policy of map acquisition. The publishers of map series sometimes issue index sheets of them which can be marked up to indicate holdings. It is necessary to be on the mailing lists of the appropriate map publishers and it is useful for some libraries to obtain also the accession lists of some of the major map libraries, for example, the library of the Royal Geographical Society. Atlases are recorded in the *BNB* and the Whitaker lists of British publications. Sheet maps are not.

Most countries now have a national cartographic survey,

but only a few libraries need to collect the maps of foreign surveys. Our national cartographic survey is the Ordnance Survey of Great Britain, to give it its full title. Northern Ireland and Eire have had their own surveys since the partition of Ireland in 1922. Because of their high standard of production, the wealth of information they include, and the wide range of scales in which they are published, a close examination of Ordnance Survey (OS) maps is strongly recommended. It is an education in cartography in itself.

Maps can be divided into two groups: general, in which the accent is on topographical features, and special, sometimes called thematic. Thematic maps are designed to show particular kinds of information, such as the incidence of rainfall, the distribution of population, or the sites of Roman remains. The OS publishes both general and thematic maps, but a good deal of special information (archaeological, for example) is incorporated in the general topographical maps.

Separate series of geological maps are published by the OS on behalf of the Institute of Geological Sciences. Land use maps, although based on OS maps, are produced and published by the independent Second Land Use Survey.

Almost all the maps of Britain published by commercial publishers, such as Bartholomew, are based on OS maps, by arrangement with the OS. It is important to remember that crown copyright in OS maps is strictly enforced.

When dealing with map queries it is necessary to understand the significance of scales, which are usually expressed as ratios. The scales used by the OS, with their interpretation in inches to the mile, are listed below. The smallest scale used by the OS, 1 : 1,000,000 (sometimes cited as 1 : 1M) is likely to be the largest used in a world atlas.

Ordnance Survey scales : table of equivalents

Small scales	
1 : 1,000,000	1 inch = 16 miles
1 : 625,000	1 inch = 10 miles
1 : 250,000	1 inch = 4 miles
1 : 63,360	1 inch = 1 mile
1 : 50,000	1¼ ins. = 1 mile
Large scales	
1 : 25,000	2 ins. = 1 mile
1 : 10,000	6 ins. = 1 mile
1 : 2,500	25 ins. = 1 mile
1 : 1,250	50 ins. = 1 mile

The most familiar scale used by the OS now is 1 : 50,000, used for its popular 'Landranger' maps of Britain. These succeeded the long familiar 'one-inch' series in the early 1970s. The one-inch scale is now used only for a small number of 'Tourist' maps of selected regions.

Since World War II the OS has used an arbitrary metric grid on its maps, a reference system known as the National Grid. This is fully explained by J.B. Harley in the OS official manual *Ordnance Survey maps*, noted below.

For the benefit of local authorities, the OS large-scale maps are being 'digitised', which means that all the information on these maps is being fed into a computer, where it can easily be kept up-to-date. A print-out can be made on any scale the user wants.

The present interest in historical studies has created a demand for maps drawn in previous centuries, some of which (for example, estate plans) were not published. As a result, many facsimiles of old maps have been published, among them early OS one-inch maps which have been reprinted, in an edited edition, by David & Charles. Local studies have also stimulated the compilation of bibliographies of old maps.

Not all maps in a library will be in the map collections. Some useful thematic maps will be in monographs and reports, and even in periodicals. In special collections it may be possible to keep an index of these. Otherwise there is a danger of overlooking, say, a map of the present vineyards of England, or a map illustrating the railway history of Leicestershire.

Atlases

The advantages of atlases are that the maps can be kept in sequence and can be more conveniently indexed than a collection of sheet maps. They can also be augmented more easily with explanatory texts. Their prime difficulty is that they cannot cope with large scales without becoming unwieldy in size, using folding maps, which are tiresome, or showing only a small area of country on each page. A large collection of atlases is an impressive sight. It can also be confusing owing to the recent trend of publishing thematic atlases in which the text is more apparent than the maps. One wonders, for example, whether the *Atlas of earth resources*, (Mitchell Beazley, 1979) is rightly called an atlas at all.

The following brief selection of atlases, all of which have won general approval, will show how much can be done with maps in volume form, despite the restriction of size.

Times atlas of the world: comprehensive edition. 6th edn, (Times Books, 1980). This is acknowledged to be the finest contemporary atlas of the world. The Foreword should be read in full before examining the maps, which were produced by Bartholomew of Edinburgh. Note the arrangement (Europe is not given priority), the use of fairly large scales (some maps are 1 : 1M or larger), the clear type face and the skilful use of colour. The number of places indexed (about 210,000) may seem small for a world atlas, but compare this number with other atlases. (The Foreword makes the pertinent remark 'Locating a place is often easier than spelling its name'.)

Ordnance Survey atlas of Great Britain. (Ordnance Survey and Country Life Books, 1982). A bound set of the OS 1 : 250,000 (¼ inch) Routemaster maps, with an authoritative text on the geography of modern Britain and Britain in the past, illustrated with small thematic maps of Britain prepared by Clyde Surveys Ltd. A student's atlas.

Shepherd's historical atlas. 8th edn, (G. Philip, 1976). A standard atlas covering world history from 1450 BC to the present century. Compare this with *The Times atlas of world history* edited by Geoffrey Barraclough (Times Books, 1978), in which the maps have to fight the text for space and too often lose.

AA Greater London street atlas. 3rd edn, (Automobile Association, 1981). A good example of street maps in atlas form (scale 1 : 2000) trying fairly successfully to meet the needs of all kinds of users.

Gazetteers

The term gazetteer has two meanings. It can mean either the index to an atlas or a separately published reference work which provides information on places — of the world, of a particular country, or a region — under their names in alphabetical order. The latter type is sometimes called a geographical dictionary, but, as Harold Nichols observes, this is a misleading use of the term. 'Place' can mean a number of things: a physical feature, a country, a town, a village, a country house, an administrative area and several other things. A gazetteer can be useful in association with a map, in that it locates places. It is also likely to be useful in its own right as a source of varied information. The more elaborate gazetteers will give for a town a miscellany of information of probable use to visitors or intending residents.

As it is costly to produce a detailed, accurate gazetteer, the best of them are revised too infrequently. We live in a rapidly changing world and gazetteers, like encyclopedias, have difficulty in keeping pace with it. A gazetteer of the world should take note of the changes in place-names which occurred in Algeria when it achieved independence in 1962. A gazetteer of Great Britain should take note of the drastic changes in local government authorities which took place in 1974.

Unfortunately, what was once the finest gazetteer of the world is now much in need of revision, but used with discretion it can still be helpful and it is worth examining to see how informative and encyclopedic a gazetteer can be. I refer to the *Columbia Lippincott gazetteer of the world* (New York: Columbia University Press, 1962). The best world gazetteer at present is *Webster's new geographical dictionary* (Springfield, Mass.: Merriam, 1972). A good feature of the Merriam-Webster series of reference books is that they all indicate pronunciation.

The Times index gazetteer of the world (*The Times*, 1965) also needs revision, but it claims to include more places than any other world gazetteer. It is not encyclopedic, however; it only provides locations. In part, it is an index to *The Times atlas of the world mid-century edition*, but it locates (by latitude and longitude) many places not in *The Times atlas*.

For Great Britain there is the *Bartholomew gazetteer of Britain* (Edinburgh: Bartholomew, 1977). Something which librarians learn from experience is that a new reference work does not always supersede an old one. Although the *Gazetteer of the British Isles* (9th edn, Bartholomew, 1963) is in many respects out-of-date, it includes many more entries on Britain than the *Bartholomew gazetteer of Britain*, and not all of the excluded entries are only of historical interest.

Further reading

There are many books and pamphlets on the nature and use of maps. Although they lack the benefit of coloured illustrations the following books are recommended: G.R.P.

Lawrence, *Cartographic methods* (Methuen, 1971) and A.G. Hodgkins, *Understanding maps: a systematic history of their use and development* (Folkestone: Dawson, 1981). The second work combines a history of cartography with explanations of cartographic techniques.

There are several good essays on 'The elements of maps' in *Map librarianship: readings* compiled by Roman Drazniowsky (Metuchen, NS: Scarecrow Press, 1975).

A useful survey of the major atlases, map series and gazetteers will be found in *Higgens*, chapter 11 'Maps, atlases and gazetteers' by Harold Nichols.

A brief but helpful introduction to the history and current map series of the Ordnance Survey will be found in the *Ordnance Survey atlas of Great Britain* (Ordnance Survey and Country Life Books, 1982) pp.14–16. The best and fullest source of information on the publications of the Ordnance Survey is J.B. Harley, *Ordnance Survey maps: a descriptive manual* (Southampton: Ordnance Survey, 1975). Unfortunately, the map specimens are too small and they are separated from the text they illustrate.

Free publicity on Ordnance Survey maps may be obtained from the Ordnance Survey, Romsey Road, Maybush, Southampton SO9 4DN.

On the use of maps for historical research see J.B. Harley, *Maps for the local historian: a guide to the British sources* (National Council of Social Service, 1972).

The principles and practice of map librarianship are explained in Harold Nichols, *Map librarianship* (2nd edn, Bingley, 1982), the only British textbook on the subject.

The *Cartographic Journal* (British Cartographic Society), half-yearly, includes notes on recent maps and atlases.

References

1   Skelton, R.A., *Decorative printed maps of the 15th to 18th centuries*, revised edn, Spring Books, 1965, p.1.
2   Hodgkins, A.G., *Maps for books and theses*, Newton Abbot: David & Charles, 1970.

21 Patent specifications and standards

This chapter deals briefly with two types of sources of information which belong to the literature of technology. Patent specifications are far less widely available in libraries than standards and therefore no more is done here than to explain what they are and why, in a small number of libraries, they form a vital part of the stock.

Patent specifications are often referred to simply as 'patents', although properly speaking a patent is a legal document (nowadays usually a mere certificate) by which the state gives to the owner of an invention the exclusive right to use it, or sell it, for a set number of years. A *patent specification* is the formal description of a patent, published by the government's patent office. Patent specifications are important in a small number of industrial special libraries, which collect them in their own fields of interest, and in the few public technical libraries (a smaller number than there used to be) which are repositories for them. A repository library receives copies of all British patent specifications, and sets of foreign specifications in relation to local demand. Patent specifications are now published in vast numbers. (The British Patent Office publishes more specifications than HMSO publishes books and pamphlets.) In their unabridged form they are great space eaters in libraries obliged to stock them, but this problem is likely to be overcome before long.

The more obvious use of patent specifications is by inventors (using the term in its institutional as well as in its personal sense) and patent agents working on their behalf, who have to search patent specifications to ensure that an invention for which a patent is to be sought is really novel. But it has been argued that the value of patent specifications as sources of technical information is potentially much wider than this. Unfortunately, the obligatory legalistic form of a patent specification makes it a good deal less readable than an article in the *New Scientist*, and the official indexes of patent specifications are a further deterrent. But in the opinion of Felix Liebesny 'If the patent literature is neglected by those seeking technical information, there is

92

considerable risk that a significant amount of important information may not be retrieved'. This observation was based on the report of an investigation which suggested that 'only a very small number of patent specifications forms the bases of corresponding publications in other forms of literature such as periodical articles, books, or conference proceedings'.

Since 1980 there has been a Patents Information Network (PIN) in the UK, embracing the international collections of patent specifications at the British Library Science Reference Library, in London, and five other British libraries accessible to the public, with smaller collections in the public technical libraries of twenty provincial cities. General information on patents is published in the *PIN Bulletin* (Science Reference Library). A comprehensive patent information service is provided commercially by Derwent Publications.

A promising development in the USA has been the transfer of thousands of current US patent specifications to video discs. As explained in chapter 4 these offer a fantastic saving in space, as one small Laservision disc can record thousands of pages of print and illustrations.

Standards

Broadly speaking, standards are common to all human enterprises. They are promulgated by government departments, a wide variety of non-government institutions, and many professional associations. But if one comes across a collection in a library labelled 'Standards' they will be standards published by the independent standards institutions and government departments to regulate the manufacture and design of specific goods, and to ensure uniformity in quality, size, shape and methods of manufacture.

In their nature and number, standards are far less daunting than patent specifications. In the UK most standards are formulated by expert committees set up by the British Standards Institution, which publishes them in pamphlet form. All British Standards in force are listed numerically, with brief annotations, in the *British Standards yearbook.* New and revised Standards are listed in the monthly *BSI News.* A British Standard is usually asked for by its serial number, coupled with the year in which it was approved, for example, BS 4360 : 1979 *Weldable structural steels.*

A technical library will also have British government defence specifications and standards published in other countries. The largest standards organisation in the USA is the American Society for Testing and Materials. The American National Standards Institute approves standards, but does not formulate them.

Further reading

On patent specifications see *Grogan*, chapter 15 'Patents' and Patent Office, *Patents a source of technical information*, an excellent booklet frequently revised and obtainable free from: Science Reference Library, 25 Southampton Buildings, London WC2A 1AW. There is also a good symposium by F. Liebesny and others 'The scientific and technical information contained in patent specifications' *Information scientist*, *8* (4), December 1974, pp.165−77.

The School of Librarianship and Information Studies, Newcastle-upon-Tyne Polytechnic, has prepared a variety of 'training packages' on patent literature. These include tape-slide programmes, video cassettes and an online teaching unit.

On the historical value of patent specifications see Frank Taylor, 'Patents and the local historian', *Local Studies Librarian, 1* (3), Winter 1982, pp.4−6.

On standards see *Grogan*, chapter 16 'Standards'.

22 Dictionaries of quotations and concordances

There are times when literature (in the exalted rather than the workaday sense) has to be added to the repertoire of sources of information. This happens when readers wish to identify, check the texts of, or precisely locate, lines by poets and passages by prose writers. Two types of reference works are helpful here: *dictionaries of quotations* and *concordances*.

Dictionaries of quotations

A dictionary of quotations assembles striking observations from many sources. Not all of them are works of literature, and not all of the persons quoted are authors, and if they are they may not be at all eminent. 'They also serve who only stand and wait' was written by a great poet (Milton). 'We had better wait and see' was a remark often made by a former British Prime Minister (Herbert Asquith). Both quotations are in the *Oxford dictionary of quotations* (3rd edn, Oxford University Press, 1979).

All dictionaries of quotations identify the authors of quotations, but some are more precise than others in giving locations. Prose presents problems, but with poetry and poetic drama precision is easy, except when there are variant versions. Dictionaries vary not only in scope and precision but in arrangement. Some are arranged alphabetically by authors, some chronologically by authors, and other alphabetically by subjects.

The use of a dictionary of quotations to find appropriate *obiter dicta* for a speech or a publication is regarded by some people as tantamount to cheating at cards. But a librarian would be wise to provide not only dictionaries arranged by authors, such as the *Oxford dictionary of quotations*, but the *Home book of quotations* edited by Burton Stevenson (10th edn, New York: Dodd, Mead, 1967; published in Britain as *Stevenson's book of quotations* Cassell, 1974), which is arranged by subjects.

Because striking sayings are constantly being coined, and

because the compilers of dictionaries differ in their criteria of selection, the number of dictionaries of quotations has become embarrassingly large. Inevitably there is overlap. But with dictionaries of quotations, as with language dictionaries, librarians must acknowledge the fact that some readers have established loyalties. These extend not only to individual dictionaries but to particular editions of them. Some users of the *Oxford dictionary* resented changes made in the third edition.

There is an increasing number of specialist dictionaries of quotations. Few of these become standard, but two recent examples are very likely to. They are *The Oxford book of aphorisms* chosen by John Gross (OUP, 1983) and *The dictionary of biographical quotation* edited by Justin Wintle and Richard Kenin (Routledge & Kegan Paul, 1978) which brings together witty and perceptive remarks on the famous of all ages.

These remarks on dictionaries of quotations end with a quotation which does not appear in any dictionary of quotations: Paul Minet, 'Quotations are made standard, not by their authors, but by their quoters', *Antiquarian Book Monthly Review, 9* (11), November 1982, p.436.

Concordances

According to the *Oxford English dictionary*, a concordance is 'an alphabetical arrangement of the principal words contained in a book, with citations of the passages in which they occur'. This definition is fine as far as it goes, but it needs enlarging. There are many books, but few justify the arrangement of the principal words in them. Most concordances are indexes to the writings of individual authors of classic status. Poets are the most favoured, but there are a few exceptions. For example, there is a concordance to the plays of Congreve, which are mainly in prose. The most familiar concordances (they are not found only in libraries) are those of the various English translations of the Bible. The best-known example is Alexander Cruden, *A complete concordance to the Old and New Testaments with a concordance to the Apocrypha*, first published in 1737 and still in print, although in a revised edition.

In view of their limited use (they augment dictionaries of quotations, but are referred to much less) concordances to individual authors are more numerous than one would expect,

But over the past twenty years the labour of compiling them has been reduced with the aid of computers. An obvious example of a computer aided concordance (obvious when you see it) is Stephen Maxfield Parrish and James Allan Painter, *A concordance to the poems of W.B. Yeats* (Ithaca, N.Y.: Cornell University Press, 1963), based on the Variorum edition of Yeats' poems.

A matter which some librarians overlook is that a concordance should be shelved next to the particular edition of the work, or works, it indexes. Apart from the Bible, this observation applies especially to the works of Shakespeare, which exist in several modern editions.

Besides their use in locating words and passages, concordances to the works of authors can be used by scholars to study their vocabularies and phraseology.

Further reading

There is nothing of importance to read on dictionaries of quotations at large. There is a learned disquisition on concordances in *ELIS*, volume 5 (1971) by Roberto Busa, pp.592—604.

On quotations there are two items which are interesting, if not important: 'To quote or not to quote' in James Agate, *An anthology* edited by Herbert Van Thal (Hart-Davis, 1961) pp.115—8, and Hesketh Pearson, *Common misquotations* (Hamish Hamilton, 1934), a little book undeservedly forgotten.

23 Illustrations

A term which has come into use in recent years is 'picture librarianship', which has been described as 'an extension of librarianship rather than a separate branch'.

Picture librarianship is not new, but because there is now an appreciable number of special libraries and special collections involved in it, it has lately become the subject of several books and many articles, as it deserves to be.

The problem of providing information visually, when words alone are insufficient, is common to all libraries. It was appreciated in public libraries years ago, when academic and special libraries were few. Thus, at the beginning of the century L. Stanley Jast, librarian of Croydon, suggested that public libraries should initiate or support local photographic surveys. Birmingham Central Library built up good collections of photographic slides and mounted illustrations for loan long before the local schools had 'resource centres'.

Providing illustrations appropriate to particular requests, especially when wanted urgently, as for example by newspaper editors, or television producers, is usually a challenge, under any circumstances. Without special collections of illustrations to draw upon it is likely to be an impossibility.

Good illustration collections today must be multi-media. Organised printed sources can still be useful, but they have to be augmented with photographic prints, slides, videotapes, videodiscs and so forth.

Illustrations are a type of source of information which cannot be helpfully discussed in a small space. They call for special knowledge and also considerable diligence as there are not only several physical forms, but an extraordinary number of firms and institutes publish them. They include museums, art galleries, government departments and commercial and industrial firms, as well as specialist publishers.

There are a few aids to acquiring illustrations, for example Hilary Evans and Mary Evans, *Picture researchers handbook* (2nd edition, Saturday Venture, 1979) an international directory of sources.

Further reading

Hilary Evans, *Picture librarianship* (Bingley, 1980) is a fairly good introduction to the organisation of a picture collection, but the various types of visual information are dealt with more thoroughly in the admirable *Art library manual* edited by Philip Pacey (Bowker, 1977), a volume which shows better than any other textbook on librarianship how various in physical form the stocks of libraries providing an efficient reference and information service must be nowadays. See also Helen P. Harrison (ed.), *Picture librarianship* (Library Association, 1981), particularly the Editor's Introduction and Part 2, which is devoted to 'Case studies and surveys of picture libraries'.

24 Printed ephemera

A certain recording of *Perpetuum Mobile* by Johann Strauss ends with the conductor saying 'And so on, and so on . . .', a phrase which could well be used to end this survey of types of printed sources of information. Many of the types not dealt with previously belong to printed ephemera, a fascinating group of publications, if we may call them so, which have lately received a good deal of attention.

'Ephemera' is yet another term whose definition is the subject of argument. John Johnson, former Printer to the Oxford University Press, whose magnificent collection of printed ephemera was acquired in 1968 by the Bodleian Library, said of the term: 'It is difficult to describe it except by saying that it is everything which would ordinarily go into the waste paper basket that is not actually a book'.

The publicity that has been given to the Johnson Collection since it was acquired by the Bodleian has stimulated interest in ephemera generally and in the other collections of it which exist in various libraries and museums around the country.

The essential point is that ephemera are not merely of casual nostalgic interest; they can be of unique value to researchers in many areas of social history. Examples of printed ephemera which may be found in libraries – not necessarily as separately organised collections – are invitations, posters, theatre programmes, electioneering literature, timetables, postcards, greetings cards, 'street literature', railway tickets, printed labels, cigarette cards and postage stamps.

Librarians have not been oblivious to the value of ephemera, as reference to the stocks of local studies collections will testify. The important thing about printed ephemera is that it should be collected while it is still current. A well-known librarian who realised this was H.M. Cashmore (1882–1972), former city librarian of Birmingham, whose personal collection of ephemera is now in Birmingham Central Library.

There is now an Ephemera Society, which publishes a

100

journal called *The Ephemerist*. There is also a regular 'Ephemera' feature in the monthly *Antiquarian Book Monthly Review*.

Further reading

The scope of printed ephemera is so wide that it is difficult to survey it all in one volume. The best introduction to the subject, Alan Clinton, *Printed ephemera: collection, organisation, access* (Bingley, 1981) illustrates its value by concentrating on a few particular types, for example, postage stamps and pictures of domestic appliances. See also John Lewis, *Collecting printed ephemera* (Studio Vista, 1976).

The John Johnson Collection is briefly surveyed by John Feather 'The sanctuary of printing: John Johnson and his Collection', *Art Libraries Journal, 1* (1), Spring 1976, pp. 23—32 and Thomas Laquer, 'The John Johnson Collection in Oxford', *History Workshop*, no. 4, Autumn 1977, pp. 82—5.

At the time of writing, a promising new book on ephemera, by a well-known authority on local studies, was in the press: C. Makepeace, *Ephemera* (Aldershot: Gower, 1984).

25 Theses (dissertations)

Theses, or dissertations (many regard these terms as synonymous) are of greatly varying worth as sources of information. When a thesis is accepted it means that its author has demonstrated, to the satisfaction of his university, that his ability to discover, assess, select and present information and furnish appropriate judgements and theories novel in themselves, or in their presentation, is of a reasonable standard. The trouble with theses is that although their authors may well have abilities deserving public acknowledgment in the form of a degree or diploma, the theses themselves may be of little interest or value to outsiders. This has become painfully evident since World War II. There are now too many students chasing too few subjects worthy of attention for reasons other than the academic exercise involved in grappling with them.

The fact that a thesis has been accepted does not mean that it is altogether admirable. So even when a thesis deals with a mainstream subject it is unlikely to be formally published. If it is (and very few theses are) it is likely to be in a revised form. Many theses, even doctoral dissertations nowadays, are written by young scholars who lack maturity in style if not in thought. A further, and very obvious point, is that literary airs and graces are not encouraged when writing a thesis. From an informational point of view this is an advantage, but sometimes one wishes that the style matched the theme. It is only too evident that when writing a thesis one can be dull about Dickens and boring about Byzantine art.

But to be fair, there is some gold among the dross, and anyone embarking upon a thesis should know what has already been done on that subject. Therefore, the texts of all theses should be accessible and their bibliographical control should be thorough. Until the middle of this century both control and accessibility were unsatisfactory, especially in the UK. But thanks to Aslib and the British Library there has been much improvement in the UK since P.D. Record published his critical review of the situation in *A survey of thesis literature in British libraries* (Library Association, 1950).

The main source of information on the more recent British theses is *Index to theses accepted for higher degrees by the universities of Great Britain and Ireland and the Council for National Academic Awards*, 1950– , (Aslib, 1953–), originally annual but now published half-yearly. This is a classified list, but without abstracts. A further disadvantage, which the *Index* makes clear, is that access to theses depends on the regulations of the relevant universities.

In the USA, the production of doctoral dissertations alone has risen to about 50,000 a year. Copies of about 80 per cent of these are available for purchase, either in microfilm or Xerox photocopies, and abstracts of all those available thus are published in *Dissertation abstracts international*, A: *The humanities and social sciences*, B: *The sciences and engineering* (Ann Arbor, Mich.: University Microfilms International, 1938–) published monthly. The same firm also publishes quarterly a third series, C: *European abstracts*, 1974– .

The British Library Lending Division systematically acquires British and foreign theses, mostly in microfilm. Its British acquisitions are listed in *British reports, translations and theses received by the British Library Lending Division*, (Boston Spa, Yorkshire: British Library Lending Division, 1981–) published monthly with annual cumulations.

Theses on librarianship are collected by the British Library Association Library. Details will be found in its monthly journal *CABLIS*.

Further reading

Theses and their bibliographical control are dealt with in Donald Davinson, *Theses and dissertations as information sources* (Bingley, 1977). The bibliographical control of theses is also dealt with by Donald Davinson in his *Bibliographic control* (2nd edn, Bingley, 1977) chapter 10 'Theses and research in progress'. There are shrewd observations on the value of theses in the *Art library manual* edited by Philip Pacey (Bowker, 1977) chapter 11 'Theses' by Trevor Fawcett.

Readers of this book who themselves hope to write theses will find good advice of general application in George Watson *The literary thesis: a guide to research* (Longman, 1970).

Part 3: The bibliographical sources

Introduction

The object of this part of the manual is to explain the nature and importance of bibliographic control and describe the main types of enumerative bibliographies. To keep it within reasonable bounds, and to focus attention upon the more important types of bibliographies, the bibliographic control of the more specialised information sources has been dealt with in the chapters on them in Part II. This applies to government publications, maps and theses.

26 Enumerative bibliography and bibliographic control

Bibliography is the most overworked term in a librarian's vocabulary. It has one of the longest entries in *Harrod's librarian's glossary and reference book* (5th edn, Aldershot: Gower, 1983) and Roy Stokes has devoted an entire book to the explanation of its several aspects: *The function of bibliography* (2nd edn, Aldershot: Gower, 1982). The basic difficulty is that bibliography is used for two different activities:

(a) The study and detailed description of books as material objects. This is *analytical and descriptive bibliography*.
(b) The listing of books. This is *enumerative bibliography*, otherwise known as *systematic bibliography*.

Although dictionaries define bibliography in relation to books, in practice it is concerned with all printed documents, including those printed but not published. Our concern is with *enumerative bibliography*. The recent extension of this term to embrace the new non-print media makes bibliographers (and a few librarians) wince, but this usage is certain to become standard.

To be precise, our concern is not merely with the listing of printed documents, particularly published documents, but with the *effective* listing of them so that they may be traced readily by authors, titles, and subjects, and also by forms and series, whenever this is desirable. This helpful listing we call *bibliographic control*. One frequently quoted definition of this term is 'Effective access to information through bibliographies', but this ignores the fact that we need also effective listing of novels, short stories, plays, poems and *belles lettres*. (It is rather hard to have to call a printed edition of *Pride and Prejudice* a 'document', but in the world of enumerative bibliography a cool mind is more important than a warm heart.)

If for any distinctive body of printed literature — of a country, a subject, or a physical or literary form — we can easily find complete and accurate information on all the items which may be asked for we say that the bibliographic control for that group of documents is good. For reasons to be noted later, bibliographic control is seldom perfect, even when it is exerted over a subject of narrow extension, such as 'the public lending right', or the publications of an author who died some years ago, such as Sir Arthur Conan Doyle.

Bibliographic control would be difficult enough if it were concerned only with writings printed as separate entities. But it is concerned also with those published as parts of separate publications — articles in periodicals and chapters or sections in books with multiple contributors. Needless to say, these concealed contributions to knowledge, or literature, may be of great value, but might be overlooked when they would be of particular use were it not for the initiative and industry of bibliographers.

The history of bibliographic control

The history of bibliographic control, which need only be sketched broadly here, is more interesting than may be supposed, especially when it concerns the literature of important subjects such as medicine,[1] and the work of individual bibliographers, such as the unfortunate Robert Watt.[2]

The outstanding fact which emerges from the history of enumerative bibliography is that until the present century, far too little attention was paid to bibliographic control, although this was due more to lack of financial resources than lack of interest. Over the past 200 years, when publications have been numerous, it has not been easy to sustain even the publication of necessary book-trade bibliographies. The striking developments which have taken place in bibliographic control during the present century have been due to a variety of agencies. One reason for the improvement which has taken place has been the 'literature explosion' in the pure and applied sciences. The need for thorough bibliographic control in the humanities has been well appreciated by those intimately associated with them, such as historians, musicologists and literary scholars, but these potential users of bibliographies have often been obliged to produce their own, usually from slender resources. The free flow of bibliographic information on the published literature of science, technology and medicine is another matter. Competition between firms and the industrial, scientific and medical welfare of countries, have called for rigorous and continuous bibliographic control in these areas.

It was not until after World War II that efficient bibliographic control began to develop on a broad front. This is partly due to the influence and example of UNESCO. In November 1950, when UNESCO was only five years old, it held a notable Conference on the Improvement of Bibliographical Services in Paris which urged that all member states should give 'early consideration to the publication of current national bibliographies' and gave sensible advice on what should be done. It happened that, in January of the same year, the *British national bibliography* began publication. This, also, was a landmark in the history of bibliographic control.

A more recent landmark was the inauguration by IFLA (the International Federation of Library Associations and Institutions) in 1974 of a programme for Universal Bibliographic Control (UBC) which will be explained in chapter 27.

By this time, some of the limitations of bibliographic control through printed bibliographies were being overcome by the use of online computerised bibliographic records (databases), an important development which is clearly going to affect every important serial bibliography before long, although the printed versions may continue to be published for some years.

Although bibliographical work in the humanities cannot draw on industrial, or even on government funds, useful work is now being done all the same, as will be indicated in later chapters.

In short, bibliographic control is being strengthened, or inaugurated, on many fronts. But in enumerative bibliography, as in most of man's endeavours, new problems are overtaking new solutions. There was a time when publication involved the use of a printer. Today, this is not necessarily so. Anyone with access to a typewriter and duplicator can publish.

The factors in bibliographic control are subject, form (physical and literary), place, time, scope (a bibliography may be selective or exhaustive) and the amount of detail given in the individual entries. This means that the potential number of bibliographies is enormous. But in practice one has to make limitations, especially with regard to bibliographies for separate publication, although reference to almost any issue of the *BNB* will show that small-scale bibliographies on a number of topics do get published.

Where do bibliographies come from?

Although bibliographies are essential aids and guides to the tracing and identification of publications, and the discovery of information in them, the market for bibliographies is not very large. It is an institutional more than a personal market, with libraries (particularly) and book-shops as the chief purchasers. Secondly, the compilation of bibliographies, which involves close attention to detail, is time consuming, and therefore costly to commission. Not surprisingly, therefore, few commercial publishers are interested in bibliographies and very few specialise in them. Among the exceptions are Whitaker & Sons (London), H.W. Wilson (New York) and R.R. Bowker (New York). Most bibliographies are published by non-profitmaking organisations: government departments and institutions, learned and professional societies, universities and libraries with outstanding research collections.

From the publishers of bibliographies we turn to their compilers. Today, the major bibliographies have to be produced by teams, but individual bibliographers still have scope in the production of small-scale subject and form bibliographies, and almost all author bibliographies are the work of single bibliographers. The late Theodore Besterman was one of the last bibliographers who dared to tackle a large-scale bibliography single-handed. He was unwise to do so. Besterman's *World bibliography of bibliographies* (4th edn, Lausanne: Societas Bibliographica, 1965–6, 5 vols) could have been much more useful had Besterman only shared its compilation with others. Its obvious defects are that it is not evaluative, and it is restricted to separately published bibliographies.

Although the general standard of concealed bibliographies is low, some of them are excellent. Concealed bibliographies include those appended to monographs, especially textbooks, and bibliographies published in learned periodicals.

Assessing bibliographies

Many librarians probably regard bibliographies as the most important tools of their trade. They soon become expert in assessing them. This is partly because the features of a bibliography are boldly exposed, so that many of its virtues and defects are soon discovered. If a bibliography is arranged by authors' names when subject classification with an author index would be more helpful; if important details such as publishers' names and dates of publication are missing; if non-descriptive titles are not explained; and if there is no indication of the purpose the bibliography is intended to serve, a librarian of only modest experience will soon perceive its defects and look for something better.

Some defects in bibliographies are due to lack of sufficient financial resources; others to lack of imagination and commonsense. Librarians can be as bad at bibliographical work as any, despite their training and constant use of bibliographies. I have seen 'reading lists' compiled by librarians as poor as those compiled by academics.

It should be added that the passage of time undermines the value of even the best bibliographies. It is almost impossible to produce a 'definitive' bibliography. But if a bibliography wins favour, so that it can be revised, or supplemented, its defects will be tolerated and it will become a standard work.

Some bibliographies are so massive that they can have no use other than for reference. But there are others which, though useful for reference, are also of the right scale to encourage browsing. It is this kind of bibliography which Robert L. Collison must have had in mind when he wrote:

> There is something very satisfying in handling a well-constructed bibliography: the care and enthusiasm with which the bibliographer has applied himself to his task is reflected in the thoughtful annotations, the ample cross-references and the careful selection of material, so that the user is constantly being directed to new ideas and his conception of his subject enriched by the indication of new fields as yet unexplored.[3]

A splendid example of a one-volume bibliography which, for about twenty years, has given help and pleasure to many, is F. Seymour Smith, *An English library* (5th edn, Deutsch, 1963), an annotated guide to the English classics, and their best current editions, for the general reader. Seymour Smith, like Robert Collison and A.J. Walford, was a librarian-bibliographer.

Tracing bibliographies

The bibliographic control of bibliographies presents difficulties, for the following reasons:

(a) the total number of usable bibliographies, including concealed bibliographies, is considerable;

(b) finding out whether or not a bibliography exists on a given topic, suitable for a particular reader, and also whether it is worth while getting hold of if it is not in stock, is seldom easy;

(c) the major bibliographies are expensive to buy and house.

The bibliographic control of published bibliographies is patchy. Besterman's *World bibliography of bibliographies* is out of date. One is therefore more likely to turn to the *Bibliographic index* 1937–   (New York: H.W. Wilson; half-yearly plus an annual cumulation). This is an alphabetical subject list of separately published and concealed bibliographies, but it is not evaluative and it does not cover British periodicals. But it is worth consulting. A surprising number of separately published bibliographies turn up in the *BNB*, but they are not evaluated. The major bibliographies of current use are given a place in *Walford* and *Sheehy*, but the annotations are not always helpful enough.

One day we may have impeccable answers to all our bibliographical queries through online databanks, but that day is a long way off.

Further reading

The best short explanation of the meaning of bibliography is the article 'Bibliography' by Sir Frank Francis in the *New Encyclopædia Britannica* (1974), *Macropædia* section, vol. 2, pp.978–81.

On bibliographic control generally see Donald Davinson *Bibliographic control* (2nd edn, Bingley, 1981), chapter 1 'The meaning of bibliographic control'.

There is no better way of getting to understand the need for good bibliographic control, and the difficulty of securing it, than to undertake a little bibliographical work oneself. The mechanics are explained in A.M. Lewin Robinson, *Systematic bibliography* (4th edn, Bingley, 1979).

References

1   See, for example, Estelle Brodman, *The development of medical bibliography*, Baltimore: Medical Library Association, 1954.
2   Robert Watt (1774–1819) impoverished himself by compiling the *Bibliotheca Britannica* (1819–24).
3   Collison, Robert L., *Bibliographies: subject and national*, 3rd edn, Crosby Lockwood, 1968, p.xiii.

27 General national bibliographies

Most bibliographies are subject bibliographies. But there cannot be effective subject bibliographies unless there are wide-ranging and efficient general bibliographies. General bibliographies are extremely important as they are, with a few exceptions, national bibliographies. That is to say, they are serial bibliographies, mainly of books and pamphlets, relating to individual countries, covering all languages but keeping a particularly close watch on publications put on sale, and therefore available from bookshops.

Serial bibliographies present a problem in nomenclature. They are sometimes referred to as 'current bibliographies, but in that they can be used to find details of books published years ago, and no longer in print, they can also be regarded as 'retrospective'. For example, the well-known *Cumulative book index* (H. W. Wilson) will provide information on many American books not recently published, or currently in print, back to the year 1898.

All the national bibliographies to be mentioned later are serial bibliographies which can be used for current and retrospective information, but their retrospective use is limited to the present century, or a small part of it. Details of books published more than a decade ago are often obtained from the published catalogues of the great national libraries (see chapter 28). Occasionally, the files of old book-trade bibliographies are used, for example, the *English catalogue of books* 1801–1968 (Sampson Low, 1864–1901; Publishers' Circular, 1906–69).

The year 1950 was a landmark in the history of bibliographic control. In January the *BNB* was established. In November UNESCO held an international Conference on the Improvement of Bibliographical Services. In the *General Report* of this conference there were recommendations. Each of UNESCO's member states was urged to encourage the publication of a comprehensive series of current bibliographies of its country's publications, that is, bibliographies of all books and pamphlets published (including those not on sale), plus lists of maps, music, audiovisual materials and theses. As far as it went, the UNESCO recommendations

115

were quite sensible. But they did not go far enough.[1] Looking at the situation today, from the point of view of the main users of national bibliographies, namely, libraries and bookshops, three main types of serial bibliographies of current publications are wanted, namely:

1 Lists of new books and pamphlets, including revised editions and reprints which involve change of publisher, price, or format (particularly the release of paperback editions of books first published in hard cover).
2 Lists of all books in print.
3 Lists of books due to be published during the next two or three months.

This broad classification of current bibliographies will be used later in this chapter when dealing with the national bibliographies of the UK and the USA. First, however, it is necessary to draw attention to three things which have affected national bibliographies in recent years. The first is the elimination, owing to their cost, of multi-annual printed cumulations. The second is the increasing use of high-reduction microfiche in addition to, or in place of, printed lists. The third is the addition of International Standard Book Numbers (ISBNs) to the entries for books and pamphlets. An ISBN identifies a book, and that particular edition of it, absolutely. It can be used for book ordering and a number of other purposes. It is made up of ten digits whose significance is indicated by the following example:

The book with ISBN 0 406 55500 1

0	signifies :	the UK/USA group of publishers
406	signifies :	the name of the publishers – Butterworths
55500	signifies :	the author, title, edition, and date of the book – J. H. Baker, *Introduction to English legal history*, 1st edn, 1971
1	signifies :	a check digit which will detect an error in transcription

British national bibliographies

(a)   Serial lists of new books

The bibliographic control of new British books is largely in the hands of the British Library Bibliographic Services Division and J. Whitaker & Son. Lesser roles are assumed by the British Council and the small commercial firm of Braithwaite & Taylor. The contribution of each of these organisations is as follows.

The Whitaker bibliographies
The firm of Whitaker lists new books in the following serial publications:

'Publications of the week' in the *Bookseller*, weekly.
Whitaker's books of the month and books to come, monthly.
Whitaker's classified monthly book list, monthly.
Whitaker's cumulative book list, 1924–   , quarterly, cumulating progressively throughout the year.

The first item is an author-title list which appears at the end of Whitaker's book-trade journal, the *Bookseller*. This list is cumulated in *Whitaker's books of the month and books to come.* Since January 1983 there has been a companion publication: *Whitaker's classified monthly book list.* This has a broad classification, unlike the close classification used in the *BNB.* The entries for the books which have actually been published are cumulated again in *Whitaker's cumulative book list* whose quarterly issues cover the months January to March, January to June, January to September, and then the complete year.

The Whitaker lists provide rather terse entries for the books they record. They deal very selectively with non-commercial publications, and provide only a rough subject approach to books, relying too much on titles. On the other hand, they list books promptly and are comparatively cheap.

The BNB
The premier serial bibliography of new British books is:

British national bibliography, Council of the British National Bibliography, 1950–1974; British Library Bibliographic Services Division, 1974–   . It is published weekly with interim cumulations for January to April and May to August; annual cumulation. A microfiche retrospective edition is also available.

117

Although the Whitaker lists are useful, libraries need a more comprehensive, detailed and helpfully arranged bibliography of new British publications. The *BNB*, as it is usually known, was established to provide such a record. It is based on inspection of books deposited at the Copyright Office of the British Library Reference Division, except for the Cataloguing-in-Publication (CIP) entries, which have appeared in the *BNB* since 1977. Acquaintance with the *BNB* should begin with the Preface to its latest cumulation, as this explains its salient features.

Although wider in coverage than the Whitaker lists, even the *BNB* has to be selective in certain areas, for example, government publications. It excludes altogether sheet maps and musical scores, although the latter are covered by another British Library bibliography, the *British catalogue of music*, described below.

Since 1956, the *BNB* has provided a printed catalogue card service based on its entries, but the demand for this is falling off.

Because the *BNB*'s definitive entries are based on deposited books, which are often received by the British Library weeks after publication, these entries are not up to date. The CIP entries, based on advance information from publishers, do not altogether overcome this problem, as they do not list all books to be published. Some books announced for imminent publication are delayed. A few are not published at all. Therefore the CIP entries cannot be relied upon absolutely.[2]

Although the *BNB*'s multi-annual cumulations have had to be discontinued, the annual volumes are now made available in microfiche as well as in print.

Although the *BNB* is invaluable to librarians (and the major booksellers too) it is never free from criticism. It has been criticised of late for including CIP entries on the grounds that they are not authoritative.[3]

Music published in Britain is recorded in the *British catalogue of music*. Council of the British National Bibliography, 1957–74, British Library Bibliographic Services Division, 1974– . Three issues a year are published, the third being an annual cumulation.

This excludes British books *about* music, which are in the *BNB*, but since 1982 it has covered not only music published in the UK but all foreign music sold in the UK, and all foreign music acquired by the British Library Music Library.

Audiovisual materials, now common, are exempt from

legal deposit, but with the co-operation of the firms which produce them the British Library is now controlling them too and information is given in the *British catalogue of audiovisual materials*, British Library Bibliographic Services Division, 1979, *Supplements* 1980, 1983. The first edition of this catalogue was called 'experimental'. It was successful. It records filmstrips, film loops, transparencies and audio discs and cassettes of *educational* value. It does not list films or videotapes.

British Book News

British book news, British Council, 1950—   . This is published monthly with annual indexes. We need not only national bibliographies which list every book published (even a book which argues the earth is flat may serve some purpose — the study of delusions perhaps) but those which list the more important, with authoritative assessments. Several countries now have such lists. *British Book News* is an outstanding example. Each issue includes a broadly classified list of about 230 books, each with a short signed review by an expert. Unavoidably the entries appear late, but a library could use them profitably to check its acquisitions.

The Good Book Guide

There is a second select list of new British books which is a commercial publication: *Good book guide*, 1977—   , Braithwaite & Taylor, published quarterly. This is not so wide in coverage, or so authoritative as *British book news,* but for the general reader it is far more attractive. It is broadly classified, has anonymous but helpful annotations, is illustrated with colour illustrations of dust-jackets and includes a number of special features. Altogether it is a highly commendable attempt to provide an attractive book information service for the general reader. It is backed by a postal book-sale service.

(b)   Books in print

The bibliographies of British books in print, together with a recently established bibliography of British books which have gone out of print in the past few years, are as follows:

British books in print, Whitaker, 1965—   , annual, two vols.
British books in print: microfiche edition, Whitaker, 1978—   , monthly.
British paperbacks in print, Whitaker, 1960—   , annual.

Books now out of print 1976–1982, Whitaker, 1983, microfiche, further editions depend upon demand.

For nearly a century Whitaker's list of British books in print was published at four-yearly intervals. There is now not only an annual list but an updated monthly list in microfiche. But the latter is not so good as it should be, as obviously publishers do not co-operate enough, particularly with regard to book prices. But *British books in print* lists about 350,000 titles and its companion *British paperbacks in print* about 50,000 titles.

(c)   Books to come

There are now several good sources of information on British books due to be published in the near future:

Whitaker's books of the month and books to come, monthly.
Whitaker's classified monthly book list, monthly.
British national bibliography, British Library Bibliographic Services Division, weekly.
British book news, British Council, monthly.

For many years information on books to come (useful information for librarians to have) was derived from the publicity material distributed by individual publishers and the advertisements in the special, enlarged Spring and Autumn issues of the *Bookseller*. The latter are still worth looking at (Whitakers provide an index in these special issues to all the books advertised), but their coverage is not wide enough and their publication is too infrequent. *Whitaker's books of the month and books to come* provides brief information on books to be published about two months ahead. *British book news* in each of its monthly issues includes a broadly classified list of 'next month's books'.

The CIP entries in the *BNB*, which were mentioned earlier, are those now marked with an asterisk. The information is obtained from the publishers on standard data-sheets, and when the books have been published and deposited at the British Library, the provisional CIP entries are revised and published in the interim and annual cumulations of the *BNB*. Not all publishers are co-operating with the *BNB* in the provision of CIP entries. By 1982 only about a quarter of the books listed in the *BNB* had been reported in advance of publication. But an investigation carried out by the Centre for Catalogue Research at Bath University suggests that the CIP entries are twice as likely to be used as the basis for selecting books as non-CIP entries.[4]

120

American national bibliographies

(a) Serial lists of new books

The listing of new American books is largely in the hands of two commercial publishers with long experience of bibliographical work: H.W. Wilson and R.R. Bowker. Bowker provides a more comprehensive service, but Wilson also lists books in English published outside the USA. A select list of new books is published by the Association of College and Research Libraries.

The Bowker lists

Weekly record, New York: R.R. Bowker, 1974– , weekly.
American book publishing record, New York: R.R. Bowker, 1960– , monthly; annual and five-yearly cumulations.

The *Weekly record* is an author list, with brief descriptive notes. The monthly *American book publishing record* is broadly classed by the DC, again with brief annotations. There are author, title and subject indexes.

The Wilson list

Cumulative book index, New York: H.W. Wilson, 1898– , monthly (except August); annual cumulations.

The *CBI* is an alphabetical author, title and subject list. Its sub-title is 'a world list of books in the English language', which means that it lists books published in Canada and the UK, as well as in the USA, but it is used in British libraries mainly as a handy, well-edited bibliography of new American books. Books wholly in foreign languages are excluded.

Choice

Choice, Chicago, Ill.: Association of College and Research Libraries, 1964– , monthly (except August); monthly and annual indexes.

Although officially described as a list of new books 'for college libraries', this broad based selection (about 500 titles) can be useful in other libraries also. Each book has a short, unsigned review. The arrangement is by subject. This excellent, authoritative list deserves to be better known in the UK.

(b) Books in print

Books in print, New York: R.R. Bowker, 1948– , annual, three author vols, three title vols.

Books in print microfiche edition, New York: R.R. Bowker, monthly; also available quarterly.
Subject guide to books in print, New York: R.R. Bowker, 1957– , annual, three vols.

These massive bibliographies list over half a million books published and distributed in the USA. The *Subject Guide*, which has no equivalent in the UK, lists books alphabetically under Library of Congress subject headings.

(c) Books to come

Forthcoming books, New York: R.R. Bowker, 1966– , bi-monthly.
Subject guide to forthcoming books, New York: R.R. Bowker, 1967– , bi-monthly.

This type of national bibliography was pioneered by Bowker.

Books in English

Books are published in English around the world and the need to be able to trace all of them without difficulty is now recognised. As the compilers of reading lists are often unwilling to give more information about a book than its author and title, the origins of a book with an English title can be a matter of speculation. But a thorough listing of books in English has a number of uses.

No serial bibliography covers exhaustively books published in English around the world, but between them the following four bibliographies must cover a good percentage:

(a) New books in English

Books in English, British Library Bibliographic Services Division, 1972– , ultrafiche, bi-monthly, cumulating progressively throughout the year.
Cumulative book index, New York: H.W. Wilson, 1928– , monthly (except August); annual cumulations.

Books in English is an author-title list of every new book in the English language catalogued by the *BNB* and the Library of Congress. It is published only in high reduction microfiche.

As mentioned earlier, the *CBI* lists not only books published in North America, but in Great Britain as well.

Although it has been published since 1898, the *CBI* did not list British books until 1928. This is a well produced bibliography, although its coverage of British books does not rival the *BNB*.

Books in English in print

International books in print, Munich: K.G. Saur, 1979– , two-yearly.

This new bibliography lists books in English published around the world, in about 100 countries, *other than in Britain and the USA*. There are nearly 100,000 titles.

Universal bibliography

Although our main concern in this chapter is with national bibliographies, something must be said about bibliographic control at international level. It exists most successfully in the sciences, where there are several efficient serial bibliographies. But it is desirable that there should be overall bibliographical co-operation internationally.

One of the few well-known events in the history of enumerative bibliography is the valiant attempt made by two Belgian scholars, Paul Otlet and Henri La Fontaine, in the early years of this century, to create a universal classified bibliography of books and important periodical articles. Although millions of entries were accumulated on cards at the headquarters of the scheme, in Brussels, the venture failed through lack of international financial support, but out of it came the Fédération Internationale de Documentation and the Universal Decimal Classification.

The Universal Bibliographic Control (UBC) programme sponsored by IFLA, and inaugurated in 1974, is far more realistic, as it is based on the recognition of the fact that effective bibliographic control must begin within individual countries, and that the exchange of bibliographical information between them is facilitated if there is international agreement on bibliographical description. The progress being made in UBC is scarcely noticed by the majority of librarians, but it continues steadily.

Further reading

Once the pattern of bibliographic control of British and American books is understood it is better to examine the bibliographies themselves than to seek further writings about them. This advice is all the more pertinent because changes in existing national bibliographies, and the publication of new ones, are more frequent than they used to be. But the following books and articles are recommended:

Davinson, Donald, *Bibliographic Control*, 2nd edn, Bingley, 1981, chapter 4 'The approach to universal bibliographic control – national biographies'.

Linford, J.E., 'Books in English', *Library Association Record, 74* (1), January 1972, p.9.

There are two useful sources of information on the past and present activities of the British Library Bibliographic Services Division:

Jeffreys, A.E., 'The first ten years of the British Library – 4: Bibliographic Services Division', *Library Review*, vol. 32, Spring 1983, pp.67–75.

The file of the *British Library Bibliographic Services Division Newsletter*, 1976– , quarterly.

On the IFLA UBC programme see:

Anderson, Dorothy, *Universal bibliographic control: a long term policy: a plan for action*, Pullach bei München: Verlag Dokumentation, 1974.

The *ALA Yearbook* 1976 to date. The 'Review of library events' section includes a short article each year on recent progress in UBC.

References

1   See the *General report of the Conference on the improvement of bibliographical services*, November 1950, Paris: UNESCO, 1950.

2   Humphreys, Garry, 'BNB – who or what is it for?', *Refer, 2* (2), Autumn 1982, pp.3–4.

3   Dixon, G., 'Is CIP impossible?' (letter), *Library Association Record, 83* (4), April 1981, p.202.

4   Bryant, Philip, 'The use of cataloguing-in-publication in United Kingdom libraries', *Journal of Librarianship, 15* (1), January 1983, pp.1–18.

5   Sayers, W.C. Berwick, *A manual of classification*, 3rd edn, Deutsch, 1955, pp.127–8.

28 Published library catalogues

A catalogue is not a bibliography, a fact which bibliographers are at pains to emphasise. A catalogue is an orderly list of items in a library, or some distinct part of it, or of the stocks of a group of libraries. The difference between a library catalogue and a bibliography has been neatly expressed by Robert Collison thus:

> A catalogue is both more and less than a bibliography. Within the definition of its purpose a bibliography attempts to be comprehensive; thus, if it is a bibliography of the best material on a subject then, even though it is selective, it will try to include all that is really first-class, and omit anything that falls below that criteria. Similarly, if it declares its purpose to be comprehensive within certain limits, it will try to include everything that can be discovered. Such aims can never be fulfilled by a library catalogue.[1]

Nevertheless, a library catalogue can be a very useful source of bibliographical information, provided that the stock is outstandingly good and the catalogue has been well compiled. It is for this reason that published library catalogues are being considered here in juxtaposition to bibliographies. As the reference stock of any research library will show, as sources of information, bibliographies and published library catalogues are complementary.

A century ago, when printing was cheap, and most libraries were closed access (which means that the readers were not allowed to go to the shelves and had to ask the staff to get the books they wanted, or thought they wanted) almost every library published its catalogue. The average standard was not high. With open access the card catalogue came into its own and the printed catalogue almost disappeared. In recent years it has made a partial comeback (a) because we now have many special libraries with unique resources, and (b) computerised catalogues, in association with microphotography and high speed photocopying techniques, have made it feasible to publish, in full, catalogues whose bibliographical value is high, though the demand for them may be small.

The best-known examples are the catalogues of the national libraries of Britain and France and the union catalogues of the Library of Congress and other research libraries in the USA and Canada, to which can be added the smaller but widely used short-title catalogues of pre-eighteenth century British books in British and American libraries, although the latter are more important for their locations than bibliographical detail. But there is now a fair number of published catalogues of special libraries. Many of these are facsimiles of entries in the card catalogues of these libraries. The American firm of G.K. Hall has published a number of special library catalogues in this form.

National library catalogues

The catalogue of a national library is useful because it systematically collects and preserves all the nation's publications. As the library of the British Museum (now the main part of the British Library Reference Division) was not founded until 1753, and as the law of legal deposit was not rigorously enforced until the mid-nineteenth century, there are still gaps in the library's holdings of British publications. Nevertheless, its stock of British books and periodicals is unique in scope. It also has extensive collections of books from the major European countries. Consequently, the publication of its carefully compiled name catalogue has been a boon to scholars everywhere. The latest edition, known as the *BLC*, is as follows:

> British Library, *General catalogue of printed books to 1975*, K.G. Saur, 1979–84; about 360 vols; *Supplement 1976–1982*, K.G. Saur, 1983; about 50 vols. The *Supplement* is also published by the British Library in a microfiche edition.

The British Library took over also from the British Museum a subject catalogue with abbreviated entries for the acquisitions of the past century, but this is at present in arrears. Details are British Museum, *Subject index of modern works acquired* 1881–1970, British Library, 36 vols., in progress.

The National Library of Wales, which has recently published its author catalogue for the first time, has done so without the expense of printing: National Library of Wales, *Microfiche catalogue of pre-1970 publications*, Aberystwyth:

National Library of Wales, 1983, 827 fiches. The original catalogue has 900,000 cards.

Special library catalogues

One of the best-known published catalogues of a special library is the alphabetical subject catalogue of the British Library of Political and Economic Science at the London School of Economics: *A London bibliography of the social sciences*, 1931— , British Library of Political and Economic Science, 1931—68; Mansell, 1970— .

By contrast there is the recent catalogue of a library notable for its holdings of early printed books, as well as early manuscripts: *Catalogue of the Wren Library of Lincoln Cathedral: books printed before 1801*, Cambridge University Press, 1983.

Union catalogues

Union catalogues are sometimes published to aid library co-operation by inter-lending, and the provision of photo-copies. But if the publications listed are rare, the value of the published catalogues is restricted to telling scholars where they can examine volumes not available in their local lib-raries. Any union catalogue, if it is well edited, and has detailed entries, can serve as a source of bibliographical information. But for economic reasons some catalogues include only enough information to identify the publications. These are essentially location lists.

The most impressive published union catalogue (it has been described as 'the greatest book in the world') is the stupendous: *National union catalog: pre-1956 imprints*, Mansell, 1968 — . This is supplemented by the *National Union Catalog: 1956—1977*, in progress.

This is an author catalogue of books represented by the Library of Congress printed cards and many other titles from around the world. The holdings of more than 800 libraries in North America are represented.

The best-known published union library catalogues on this side of the Atlantic are the two location lists of early British printed books commonly referred to as the *STC* and *Wing*:

A.W. Pollard and G.R. Redgrave, *A short-title catalogue of books printed in England, Scotland and Ireland 1475—1640*,

W.A. Jackson and others; vol. 1 in preparation; vol. 2 *I–Z*, Bibliographical Society, 1976. (The *STC*.)

The first edition of the *STC* restricted its locations to British research libraries. The new edition covers many American research libraries also. The research libraries of both countries are covered by the first continuation of the *STC*:

Wing, Donald, *Short-title catalogue of books printed in England, Scotland, Ireland, Wales 1641–1700*, 2nd edn, New York: Modern Language Association of America, 1972– ; vol. 1 –

The work begun by these two famous location lists is now being continued to cover British books published during the eighteenth century, when the rate of publication was much greater. But the *Eighteenth-century short-title catalogue (ESTC)*, in its method of compilation and accessibility, is very different from the *STC* and *Wing*. With the assistance of the British Library, the *ESTC* has made very good progress. It is now an international project, with 600 libraries in several countries contributing to it. In 1982, the entries in the *ESTC* became accessible to searchers via BLAISE-line, one of the two bibliographical on-line services operated by the British Library.

Doubtless we shall continue to have published catalogues of some research libraries and research collections in printed form, but the future of the large-scale catalogues would seem to be with microfiche and online.

Further reading

The most useful reading on published library catalogues is the Introduction to Robert Collison, *Published library catalogues*, (Mansell, 1973).

Information on new and revised British Library catalogues is given from time to time in the *British Library News*. On the new *STC*, volume 2 see the review by Eric Clough, *Library Association Record, 78* (11), November 1976, pp.542–3. The progress of the *ESTC* is chronicled in *Factotum*, an occasional newletter about the *ESTC* published in the British Library.

References

1   Collison, Robert, *Published library catalogues*, Mansell, 1973, p.3.

29   Bibliographies of periodicals

The bibliographic control of periodicals is not so massive a task as the control of the contributions to them. Nevertheless, it has its difficulties, which do not decrease, as it is easy to produce some kind of periodical nowadays, and many small circulation periodicals exist unobtrusively. Most of them are the journals of societies and institutions. They are not advertised (for that matter, only a minority of periodicals are) and if their publishers even know about the law of legal deposit they may blithely ignore it. There are further problems which relate to periodicals generally. They are liable to appear and disappear without warning. They are likely to change their frequency, their names and their nature (for example, the *New Statesman*). As to the prices of periodicals, they are hardly worth recording in any list of current periodicals any more.

The bibliographic control of current periodicals, like the bibliographic control of books, has been mainly in the hands of commercial publishers. From the point of view of librarians and interested readers these commercially produced bibliographies, commonly called 'directories' or 'guides', are often inadequate. Their common faults are:

(a)   the exclusion of small circulation periodicals of value, such as little magazines and local periodicals;
(b)   lack of information on the nature and extra subject scope of periodicals;
(c)   lack of an effective subject classification of periodicals.

A step forward in the bibliographic control of current periodicals was the inauguration, in 1972, of an international Serials Data System, by which each periodical registered at one of the national or regional centres is given a unique eight digit International Standard Serial Number (ISSN) which can be used for ordering, compilation of union lists and other purposes.

With periodicals, as with books, it is necessary not only to compile thorough and accurate bibliographies of those published today, but to fill in the many gaps in the bibliographic control of those published in the past. The nineteenth century, the first in which periodicals existed throughout the century in large numbers, is now receiving particular attention in the USA.

A matter of some consequence, which concerns periodicals new and old, is the abbreviation of their titles, a common device in textbooks, professional manuals and in articles in learned periodicals. To take an imaginary example, if you wished to cite the *Transactions of the Portsmouth Institute of Archaeology*, it would save space, and therefore money, to abbreviate it, but there are likely snags. 'Port.' could stand for a number of towns, and 'Inst.' could mean either Institute or Institution. Fortunately, there is expert guidance on the abbreviation of periodical titles, including a British Standard, BS4148: 1970, Part 1, *Abbreviations of titles of periodicals: principles*.

Standard bibliographies of current periodicals

The following sources of information on currently published periodicals are variable in quality but widely stocked:

Ulrich's international periodicals directory, New York: Bowker, 1932– , biennial, two volumes.
Irregular serials and annuals, New York: Bowker, 1967– , biennial.
Ulrich's quarterly, New York: Bowker, 1977– , updates both of the above publications.
Willing's press guide, East Grinstead: Thomas Skinner Directories, 1874– , annual.
Benn's press directory, Tunbridge Wells: Benn Business Information Services, 1846– , (originally called the *Newspaper press directory*), vol. 1: *United Kingdom*; vol. 2, *International*, annual.
Current British journals, edited by David P. Woodworth, British Library Lending Division, 1982; frequency of revised editions not known.

All but the last of these current bibliographies are commercial publications with international coverage, of variable scope. The Bowker bibliographies are the most efficient. For each periodical they provide all the basic information, including a note if the periodical is covered by any abstracting or indexing services, and the entries are helpfully arranged under alphabetical subject headings. *Irregular serials and*

130

annuals are those published irregularly, annually, or less than once a year. Bowker records altogether about 100,000 periodicals.

By contrast, the two best-known British bibliographies of current periodicals are less helpfully compiled, although they have some advantages as sources of information on British periodicals. *Benn's press directory* is far better on British than on foreign publications. It is very informative on British newspapers. Note also its separate listing of British house journals.

The main virtue of *Willing's press guide* is its single alphabetical list of British periodicals and newspapers, although this provides minimum information. The 'Classified index' in *Willing's* is far too broad to be of much use.

Current British journals is an attempt to provide a detailed, closely classified list of current British periodicals, a bibliography which ought to be of use to librarians in periodical selection. Unfortunately, it has two serious defects. Firstly, it employs a bewildering series of arbitrary abbreviations which are not repeated on every page. Secondly, it is not frequently and regularly updated. On the other hand, the coverage is good, on the whole, and the classification by the UDC is helpful.

The first issues of new periodicals are recorded in the *BNB*, although its coverage is not exhaustive. A few of the more important new British periodicals are reviewed each month in the 'Periodicals and serials' section of *British Book News*.

Tracing non-current periodicals

Back issues of the bibliographies mentioned above may be of some use, but the following can be particularly useful:

British union catalogue of periodicals, Butterworths, 1955–8, 4 vols, *Supplement to 1960*, 1962.
Continued as:
British union catalogue of periodicals: New Periodical Titles, 1964–80, Butterworths, 1964–81, 17 vols, ceased publication.
Waterloo directory of Victorian periodicals 1824–1900, *Phase* 1, Waterloo, Ont.: Wilfrid Laurier University Press, [1976].

There are many sources of information on periodicals no longer published, but some are subject lists and others are poorly edited. In many British libraries the handiest source of information will probably be the *British union catalogue of periodicals (BUCOP)*. The original volumes (excluding *New periodical titles*) are the most useful, as they include many defunct periodicals and the entries were so well edited that they not only give inclusive dates but details of any changes of title that may have taken place. Details of locations of files cannot be altogether relied upon now, but since *BUCOP* was planned the British Library Lending Division has been established. Its holdings of old periodicals are not complete but they are quite extensive.

There are two well-known bibliographies which include concealed retrospective lists of periodicals, but they are not as helpful as *BUCOP*. One is the *British Museum general catalogue of printed books*, which has a 'Periodical Publications' section in which periodicals are awkwardly entered under the names of the towns where they were published. The other source is the *New Cambridge bibliography of English literature*, which includes in volumes 2 to 4 wide-ranging lists of periodicals of value to literary scholars. All titles listed appear in the general index (vol. 5).

For the Victorian period there is the *Waterloo directory of Victorian periodicals, Phase One*. 'Phase One' means that this is a tentative edition. The fact that, as late as 1983, we are still awaiting a definitive bibliography of the periodicals of the previous century shows how badly the bibliographic control of periodicals has been neglected.

Further reading

There is not a great deal which is worth reading and easily accessible. The best source is Donald Davinson, *The Periodicals Collection* (2nd edn, Deutsch, 1978) chapter 7 'Bibliographies of periodicals'.

On Victorian periodicals see *Victorian periodicals: a guide to research* edited by J. Don Vann and Rosemary T. Van Arsdel (New York: Modern Language Association of America, 1978) chapter II 'The bibliographic control of Victorian periodicals' by Scott Bennett.

30 Bibliographic control of the contents of periodicals

The need for bibliographic control of the contributions to periodicals, as well as of periodicals themselves, scarcely needs explanation, except perhaps for one aspect of it. Most of the articles on an established subject will appear in the periodicals expressly devoted to it, but many will also be published in periodicals that are not. The scattering of articles on a subject in 'alien' periodicals can be very wide. Important articles may turn up where they are least expected. There has been a number of investigations into this phenomenon, many of them prompted by the pioneering study of Dr S.C. Bradford (Keeper of the Science Museum Library, 1930–8) which advanced a formula of scattering always referred to as 'Bradford's law', which need not detain us. The problem of scattering can readily be demonstrated by referring to a subject of narrow extension but growing interest: British library history. Valuable articles on this subject have appeared in recent years in the *Times literary supplement, Country Life,* the *Contemporary review,* the *Book collector, History workshop,* the *Bulletin of the history of medicine,* the *Bookseller* and the *Proceedings of the Suffolk Institute of Archaeology.*

Searching for articles on a particular aspect of a subject by hopefully scanning the contents pages, or indexes of the periodicals devoted to it may, perhaps, be of some benefit, especially if the topic is new, so that the search does not have to go back a long way, but searching alien periodicals for scattered references would be an extravagant waste of time.

Tracing articles on given subjects (or by given authors) wherever they may be in the stupendous mass of periodical literature calls for union indexes, of which there are now a fair number. Those which are themselves serials are called indexing services, except where the entries include summaries of the texts, when they are called abstracting services. But before dealing with union indexes it is necessary to point to the value of the indexes to individual periodicals.

Indexes to individual periodicals

All periodicals of reference value should have their own indexes. Not all of them have. They are often unavailable for shoestring periodicals, such as little magazines and local journals. The quality of published indexes varies greatly. Some are good enough to win the approval of the Society of Indexers. Others are appallingly bad. If one takes as an acceptable standard the index to *Nature* (unusual in that it is not a volume index, but an annual index spanning several volumes) it is only too easy to find other indexes which are inferior.

When a periodical's index is good it can be useful even though the periodical is covered by an indexing or abstracting service to which the library subscribes. The reason is that indexing and abstracting services, more often than not, record contributions to periodicals selectively. Even when they record all the articles in a periodical they are likely to ignore news items, reviews and correspondence. (There are some exceptions.)

Some periodicals have, or have had, cumulated indexes in addition to the indexes to individual volumes. There is no law of probability about this. A periodical with a cumulated index, or indexes, may be of large circulation (for example, the *National Geographic Magazine*) or small (for example, the *Dickensian*). For economic reasons, cumulated indexes are becoming less common, although there is some hope that they may be revived as COM indexes — computerised indexes published in microfiche.

There is a select, international list (about 10,000 titles) of periodicals of reference value which indicates how and when they publish their indexes: *Directory of title pages, indexes and contents pages*, British Library Lending Division on behalf of the United Kingdom Serials Group, 1981. Unfortunately, a number of important periodicals are absent from this first edition, and cumulated indexes, where they exist, are not noted.

Indexing services

The need for wide-ranging bibliographies of contributions to periodicals existed long before it was met. In the English speaking world the first notable attempt to produce a union index was made a century ago by an American librarian,

William Frederick Poole, who inaugurated the index of nineteenth century British and American periodicals which bears his name: *Poole's index to periodical literature 1802 — 1906*, Boston: Houghton, 1888–1907, 7 vols.

This is a rather crude alphabetical subject index which compares unfavourably with present-day indexing services. (Try, for example, to find all the references to the 'drink problem' in Victorian England.) Poole did not provide author entries, probably because in the nineteenth century most periodical articles were either anonymous or pseudonymous. But the minority of signed articles in *Poole* can be traced in a belated supplement: *Cumulated author index for Poole's index to periodical literature 1802–1906*, Ann Arbor, Mich.: Pierian Press, 1971.

Such as it is, Poole has still to be used, as the task of producing a better subject index will be an expensive operation, and is unlikely to be undertaken until the authors of the many unsigned articles in nineteenth century periodicals have been identified, as far as this can be done. This task is now being undertaken in America in a valuable 'contents lists' type of bibliography, originated and edited by the late Professor Walter E. Houghton: *Wellesley index to Victorian periodicals 1824–1900*, University of Toronto Press, 1966–79, 3 vols, in progress.

In 1905, about the time *Poole's index* was terminated, the H.W. Wilson Company launched the *Readers' guide to periodical literature*, 1900– , the first of about a dozen selective periodical indexes now published by this firm. The Wilson indexes are expressly designed to meet the needs of American libraries, which are kept under review. This means that they are slanted towards American periodical literature and their use in British libraries is therefore restricted. But several are well-known in Britain, notably the *Applied science and technology index*, 1958– , the *Social sciences index*, 1974– , the *Humanities index*, 1974– , and the *General science index*, 1978– .

In addition to the popular but small-scale indexing services published by H.W. Wilson, America also produces several comprehensive indexes which are international in scope, among them *PAIS* (to be described later) and: *Index medicus*, National Library of Medicine, monthly; annual cumulations.

This renowned service is compiled and published in association with a pioneering online bibliographical information service called MEDLINE. This derives from the National Library of Medicine's database called MEDLARS (Medical

Literature Analyses and Retrieval System).

After a promising start in the nineteenth century, the British contribution to periodical indexing was slow to develop and is still modest in comparison with the American contribution. In the latter part of the nineteenth century the Royal Society made a brave attempt to control scientific articles published around the world with its *Catalogue of scientific papers 1800–1900*, Clay for the Royal Society of London, 1867-1902; Cambridge University Press, 1914–25. This is an author index. For financial reasons, a projected classified index had to be abandoned. The Royal Society was also the prime mover and publisher of a continuation of the *Catalogue*, a classified index of scientific articles published during the present century: *International catalogue of scientific literature 1901–1914*, Royal Society of London for the International Council, 1902–21. Unfortunately, this had to be abandoned also.

In 1915, the Library Association entered the indexing field, but for many years was unable to do more than publish a small-scale general index, and for most of its existence this was only published as an annual volume, issued several months in arrears. In 1962 this was replaced by two more frequent specialised indexes. Details of all the Library Association's indexing services are as follows:

Subject index to periodicals, 1915–22; 1926–61, Library Association.
British technology index, 1962–80, Library Association, continued with change of title:
Current technology index, 1981– , Library Association, monthly; annual cumulations; monthly and annual author indexes.
British humanities index, 1962– , Library Association, quarterly; annual cumulations. Author index in the annual volumes only.

Users of the *Current technology index* (there were objections to its unnecessary change of title) have not only the advantage of more frequent publication, but an efficient system of chain indexing. As authors count for more in the humanities than in technology, it is odd that the *BHI* should have only an annual author index. But the main purpose of periodical indexes is to reveal articles in periodicals by their subjects. These Library Association indexes are therefore typical in that they list articles under alphabetical subject headings.

136

Indexing services which list periodical articles are not always restricted to periodical articles alone. Some also list new books and pamphlets; some even list new non-print materials. This means that we have an overlap with comprehensive subject bibliographies dealt with in chapter 33. A notable example of the serial listing of periodical articles and other publications is: *Public affairs information service bulletin (PAIS)*, 1915– , New York: Public Affairs Information Service, published twice a month; annual cumulations.

There is an example of this comprehensive type of indexing service in librarianship: *Library literature* 1936– , New York: H.W. Wilson, two-monthly; annual cumulations. This is a serial continuation of the same publisher's *Library literature 1921–1932*, 1934, and *Library literature 1933–1935*, 1936.

This is an author-subject index of books, pamphlets, periodical articles, theses, films, filmstrips and microforms on librarianship and information science. Although this has some American bias, it must be recognised that far more is published on librarianship in the USA than in the UK. This is very obvious if one examines the roll of periodicals on librarianship published in the two countries.

Indexing services are essentially reference tools. As their entries are arranged under alphabetical subject/author headings, and provide no information about the articles listed other than the basic bibliographical details, and some indication of their subjects through the subject headings under which they appear, they do not encourage scanning by those users who want to monitor new periodical (or other) literature on their subjects. Scanning is encouraged, however, even without the benefit of abstracts, by serial lists of periodical articles which are contents lists.

Contents lists

Serial lists of the contents of the latest issues of the leading periodicals on a particular subject are a fairly recent addition to the bibliographies which control periodical literature. The reason for their existence is that experts in a particular subject always have an interest in, and a regard for certain periodicals on that subject and therefore like to keep an eye on what they publish. To do so in a library can be tedious and sometimes frustrating, if the latest copies have not been received, or other readers are using them. To meet the need

for information on the latest contents of important periodicals there are now serial bibliographies which consist of
facsimiles, or transcriptions, of the contents lists of periodicals in several major subjects. The best-known are those
published in the USA by the Institute for Scientific Information. One example will serve, and that is *Current contents:
Life sciences*, 1961–   , Philadelphia, PA.: Institute for
Scientific Information. It is published weekly and has subject
and author indexes. A good British example is *Contents
pages in management*, 1974–   , Manchester Business School
Library, published fortnightly with four-monthly and annual
author indexes.

Citation indexes

About twenty years ago a remarkable new type of periodical indexing service appeared in America which is more
easily understood when examined than read about: the
citation index. The first to be published was *Science citation
index*, 1961–   , Philadelphia, PA.: Institute for Scientific
Information, 1963–   , two-monthly.

The principle used in this index is one that had been used
for some years in the legal profession for the indexing of
law reports. The *Science citation index* was successful
enough to encourage the Institute to publish also the *Social
sciences citation index*, 1970–   and the *Arts and humanities
citation index*, 1978–   . Each of these indexes consists of
two alphabetical sequences, a 'Citation Index' and a 'Source
Index'. The user is instructed to:

> Look up the name of an author of a work you know to
> be relevant to your topic in the *Citation Index*. If any
> of that author's works have been cited during the period
> covered, the item will appear in the *Citation Index* with
> the citing authors listed below it. You then turn to the
> *Source Index* for details of these.

In brief, a citation index enables a researcher who has
details of one reference to a subject in which he is interested
to find others linked to it which have been published later.
Once the drill for using a citation index has been mastered
its unique value will be appreciated. Unfortunately, these
indexes are printed in tiresomely small type.

Abstracts

'Abstract' means summary, abridgement, précis. A summary can be made of any prose composition; at a pinch, even of a literary one. Our concern is with abstracts of periodicals of informational value.

Knowing that a particular periodical article exists, which may be by consulting an appropriate indexing service, might be of some help to a student or research worker, but not perhaps of much help. For example, a well-informed student of the archaeology of Roman Britain would not be taking much of a risk in asking his library to obtain a copy of an article by Professor Barry Cunliffe on the excavation of Roman remains at Bath, published by the *Antiquaries Journal*, on the strength of an entry for this article in the *British humanities index*. The author and the journal are both well known. But one cannot always augment the bare bibliographical details of an article from one's own know-ledge. In any case, the title of a periodical article, like the title of a book, can be quite uninformative, even when it is not fanciful, but tries to be descriptive. It is seldom possible to be fully descriptive in the number of words allowed for a title. As this is not so well appreciated as it should be an example is necessary. The present author once published an article under the title 'Free books in an affluent society'. It could have been called 'A historical review of the legal deposit system under the British copyright laws', but even this would have left some doubt as to the article's scope, authority, originality and the ratio between fact and com-ment, which a good abstract could make clear.

The need for abstracts of periodicals was recognised as far back as the eighteenth century, when periodical literature began to grow. But the publication of regular, wide-ranging and authoritative abstract journals is a modern phenomenon. It began in the nineteenth century. Once again we find the American bibliographers playing a major role. But Britain has made some very useful contributions. Notable examples are the scientific and technological abstract journals pub-lished by the Institution of Electrical Engineers and the agricultural series published by the Commonwealth Agri-cultural Bureaux.

The abstract services most widely known are those in the pure and applied sciences, where the literature is consider-able and still growing fast. It is here that the need for good bibliographic control is most urgent and financial support is therefore available to keep the services in operation. The following brief chronology of the dates of foundation of notable abstract journals indicates a trend one would expect: the belated establishment of abstract journals for subjects more cultural than practical.

1884 *Engineering index*
1897 The first of the Institution of Electrical Engineers' series of abstract journals.
1907 *Chemical abstracts*
1926 *Biological abstracts*
1927 *Psychological abstracts*
1947 *Excerpta medica*
1948 *Nuclear science abstracts*
1955 *Historical abstracts*
1958 *Abstracts of English studies*

There is a much greater literature on abstracting than on indexing. This is because abstracting generates more problems. Those most often discussed are these:

1 How long should an abstract be in relation to the original document?
2 Should periodicals publish abstracts of their articles? And allied with this:
3 Should the authors of articles be encouraged to provide abstracts of them for publication with the articles themselves?
4 Should abstracts be critical as well as factual?
5 Is it reasonable that an article should be independently abstracted by several abstract journals? This is related to the problem of 'slanted' abstracts, that is, abstracts which are slanted towards the interests of particular researchers.
6 How can the delays in publishing abstracts be overcome? Sometimes these can be more than six months after the publication of the original articles.

The first point, 'How long should abstracts be?', is particularly interesting as the value of an abstract to someone in search of new and vital information must depend upon its length, which is in relation to the amount of information provided. Two frequently used terms in the abstracting field relate to this problem.

Indicative abstract is a term used to describe a short summary of the original, only indicating what it is about, which its title can seldom do adequately. It is not easy to make a clear distinction between 'indicative abstract' and 'annotation'.

140

Informative abstract is a term used to describe a summary of the significant contents of the original, usable as a substitute for it where only an outline is required.

For two very good reasons, most abstracts cannot be informative. One is a matter of economics. Print is expensive. The other is that articles which depend on tabular and pictorial matter do not lend themselves to informative abstracting.

The time lag in the publication of abstracts is impossible to overcome, except to a very limited extent by having an 'express' service for selected articles regarded as being of great importance. Most abstracting has to be done part-time by experts in the subjects concerned, often without payment. On the credit side, some abstracting journals have their own document delivery service (that is, they can supply copies of the articles abstracted) and many are now produced from computerised databases which are online.

When the quantity of periodical literature is great, as in chemistry and medicine, the published abstracting services can be formidable in bulk and cost. By comparison, the abstracting services in the humanities are quite modest. Even *Historical abstracts* is small in comparison with *Chemical abstracts*.

To understand the uses and characteristics of abstract journals it is advisable to begin by examining one in a familiar subject field. An appropriate choice for many readers of this book would be *Library and information science abstracts (LISA)*, 1969– , Library Association, six issues a year. It is the successor to *Library science abstracts* 1950–68, Library Association.

Except for its small scale, and sophisticated classification, this is a typical abstract journal, in that:

1   The abstracts are more often indicative than informative.
2   Articles in foreign language periodicals are abstracted in English and are informative where possible.
3   The abstracts themselves are not cumulated, but the subject and name indexes are, annually and multi-annually.
4   The service is available for online searching. (This must now be regarded as typical of all good abstracting services.)

LISA should be compared with the H.W. Wilson Company's *Library literature* mentioned earlier. There is a marked difference in coverage between the two services.

A medium-scale abstracting service worth examining is the *Engineering index*, 1884– , New York: Engineering Index, published monthly; annual cumulations, online. Although its title suggests it is an indexing service merely, this is, in fact, an abstracting service. Like a number of other abstracting services it is not restricted to periodical articles, but covers other material, including patent specifications and research reports.

An abstracting service which all librarians have heard of, but which only a minority ever have to use, is *Chemical abstracts*. This is a massive and expensive service, but it rightly describes itself as the 'key to the world's chemical literature', and it is said to be the most widely used abstracting service in English. But to those who are unfamiliar with abstracting services it is better to examine first one or two services which are less formidable.

Abstracting services now exist for most subjects of importance, except in the humanities, where there are still some gaps. The easiest way to find out if there is a service on a particular subject is to consult *Walford, Sheehy* or *Ulrich's international periodicals directory*.

The future of printed indexing/abstracting services

Although there can be no doubt about the continued existence of indexing and abstracting services, the future of the printed versions of them is not yet clear. So far, the subscriptions to these have been only marginally reduced — about 5 per cent. There are several reasons for this, among them the delayed use of online by public libraries and the adherence of some librarians and library users to the familiar published editions.

Current awareness library bulletins

It is relevant to mention here that many libraries, especially industrial special libraries, help their readers by producing their own serial lists of new periodical articles, either as subject lists or as contents lists. Sometimes the entries have indicative abstracts. These serial lists, whatever form they take (they may include also lists of new books and so on added to the library, and news items) are often called bulletins.

142

From the readers' point of view, the advantage of these small-scale serial indexing/abstracting services, in comparison with the published ones, is that they are up to date, can be quickly scanned, and any articles listed can be obtained from the library with little delay by completing a request slip or using the interphone. From the library staff's point of view, the advantage of bibliographical bulletins is that the use made of the periodicals stocked can be monitored and information of value which might otherwise have been overlooked can be exploited. Some special libraries issue their bulletins daily.

Further reading

The literature on indexes and abstracts is large but scattered. Most of it is on abstracting. The following publications are particularly recommended:

Davinson, Donald, *Bibliographic control*, 2nd edn, Bingley, 1981, chapter 9 'Periodicals and the ancilliary aids to their use'.
Davinson, Donald, *The periodicals collection*, 2nd edn, Deutsch, 1978, chapter 8 'Guides to the content of periodicals: abstracts' and chapter 9 'Guides to the contents of periodicals: indexing services'.
Bourne, Ross (ed.), *Serials librarianship*, Library Association, 1980, chapter 16 'Abstracting and indexing services' by Stella Keenan.
Collison, Robert, *Abstracts and abstracting services*, Santa Barbara, Cal.: ABC-Clio, 1971. This is partly historical, but it includes readable chapters on the nature and writing of abstracts.
Rowley, Jennifer E., *Abstracting and indexing*, Bingley, 1982, see chapters 1, 2 and 3 in particular.
Walker, J.R.A., *Information bulletins in special libraries*, Library Association, 1966.

31 Bibliographic control of the conference proceedings

As indicated earlier in chapter 14, librarians are more concerned with the bibliographic control of conference proceedings than with the value of the proceedings themselves.

Not all conference proceedings are published, and even when they are they do not always include the texts of all the papers delivered. Some are withheld because they were disappointing; others because the speakers failed to submit the texts of their papers by the deadline for submission. Proceedings may be published long after the conferences have been held. They may be published on their own, in one or more volumes, or as a special issue of, or as a supplement to an issue of a periodical, or scattered through several issues of a periodical. Sometimes conference papers are preprinted in volume form, or separately. Not surprisingly, therefore, requests for conference papers received by librarians are apt to be confusing.

There are two bibliographical problems. The first is discovering whether or not the proceedings of a particular conference have been published. The second is discovering whether a particular paper requested has been published. In British libraries the most useful source of information on conference proceedings is the *Index of conference proceedings received*, 1964– , British Library Lending Division, published monthly with cumulations for 1964–74, 1974–8. This is an alphabetical subject index based on keywords from titles, which is not altogether satisfactory. About 16,000 conference proceedings are listed annually from around the world.

Tracing individual conference papers may depend upon whether or not they have been picked up by the abstracting and/or indexing services in the subject areas concerned. But for the 'most significant' conference proceedings in science and technology (about 3,000 a year) there is a serial bibliography which not only identifies the proceedings and lists their contents but indexes them: *Index to scientific and technical proceedings (ISTP)*, 1978– , Philadelphia, PA.: Institute for Scientific Information, published monthly with annual cumulations. This is a thorough index of subjects, authors, editors and conference locations.

Further reading

Grogan, chapter 13 'Conference proceedings' is a good survey of scientific and technical conference proceedings and their control. On the bibliographic control of conference proceedings specifically see Donald Davinson, *Bibliographic control* (2nd edn, Bingley, 1981) chapter 12 'Conference proceedings'.

32 Bibliographies of creative literature

The compilers and publishers of bibliographies cannot ignore the forms in which the items listed are produced. But whereas in some bibliographies form is subservient to other characteristics, notably subject, in others it takes precedence. A complicating factor is that there is physical form and literary form, and literary form has one pattern for informational literature and another for creative literature. The control of informational literature by its physical and literary forms has been dealt with in several other chapters of this book. In this one we are concerned with the control of creative literature. Like the legendary curate's egg, this is 'good in parts'.

We begin with English literature as a whole, for which the standard bibliography is the *New Cambridge bibliography of English literature*, (Cambridge University Press, 1974–7; 4 vols, plus an index volume). When the first edition of this was published, in 1940, it was highly acclaimed. One reviewer called it 'the bare bones of our literature'. But although for its present edition it has been not only revised, but extended to cover the literature of the first half of this century, most of its original faults remain. Firstly, it offers only 'title-a-line' lists of the writings of individual authors. On the other hand, it is bulked out with lists of books and articles about these authors, some of which are very long and include many items of little value when they were first published. There are no annotations to these writings about authors, no guidance on what is particularly worth reading. Dr R.W. Chapman, the eminent authority on Jane Austen, was invited to contribute the section on her to the first edition of the bibliography. He has recorded that his attempt to exclude 'much that seemed of small importance' from the list of writings about Jane Austen was unsuccessful. He was overruled by the editor. Fortunately for students of English literature, most of the dead literature about it has no place in the *Shorter new Cambridge bibliography of English literature*, edited by George Watson (Cambridge University Press, 1981). Both the full bibliography and its abridgement are hospitable to minor authors of merit, and

146

to the classic writers of subject literature such as scientists, travellers and historians.

In addition to these well-known Cambridge bibliographies we now have two series of semi-bibliographical reference works on English (and American) literature published by Macmillan: 'Great writers of the English language' and 'Contemporary writers of the English language', each of which includes separate volumes on poets, novelists and dramatists. The lists of authors' works are supported by short biographical and critical essays.

Considering its popularity, and its long-standing representation in the stocks of public lending libraries, one would expect a good set of bibliographies of fiction, both for students and general readers. But the situation is far from ideal. The main defect is the lack of up to date annotated bibliographies. One which used to be in general use has unfortunately not been revised for half a century: E.A. Baker and J.A. Packman, *A guide to the best fiction: English and American* (3rd edn, Routledge, 1932).

The Association of Assistant Librarians has made two contributions to the bibliography of fiction which have sold many copies, but they bear little comparison with Baker and Packman's bibliography, which derived from Dr Baker's life-long devotion to the history and bibliography of fiction and its provision in libraries.

The first and older of the two AAL bibliographies is *Sequels*, now published in two volumes. The second volume is devoted to children's books. Our concern is with Volume 1: *Adult books* (7th edn, AAL, 1982). Although non-fiction is covered, this is mainly concerned with fiction, and mostly with series (for example, the Poirot novels of Agatha Christie) rather than sequels, of which there are not very many.

The other AAL bibliography is the *Cumulated fiction index 1945–1960* (AAL, 1961) and its supplements, *1960–1969* (1970), *1970–1974* (1975) and *1975–1979* (1980). This is an alphabetical subject guide to modern fiction. Its popularity is puzzling, as it has several defects. As it is not annotated, the user is often faced with a long list of good and bad novels grouped together without distinction. The second fault is that some of the headings used are so broad that the hopeful user is overwhelmed with titles. One can be grateful for a short list on Algiers, but what can one do with the torrential lists of titles under the headings 'Detective stories' and 'Love and infatuation'? Incidentally, both of the AAL bibliographies follow the all too common practice of citing authors who always use their forenames in full with the initial letters of them. Thus, Shelley Smith becomes S. Smith, and Michael Innes becomes M. Innes.

There are several American bibliographies of fiction which have never found much favour in British libraries. This is unfortunate, as they have some merit, especially the *Fiction catalog* (9th edn, New York: H.W. Wilson, 1976; supplements).

For poetry the most important bibliography is *Granger's index to poetry* (7th edn, New York: Columbia University Press, 1982). This is an index by titles, first lines, authors and subjects of poems in anthologies, most of them American. Nevertheless, it is very useful in identifying many of the poems people are interested in. As the seventh edition does not index all the anthologies indexed in earlier editions, it does not supersede them.

We are in need of a handy, up to date, well edited bibliography of the drama. The nearest approach to this is the published catalogue of a special library which unfortunately has not been kept up to date: *The player's library* (2nd edn, Faber, 1950), *Supplements* (1951, 1954, 1956). This is the catalogue of the British Drama League.

One day, perhaps, the British Library Bibliographic Services Division will turn its attention to the bibliographic control of creative literature. There is much to do.

33 Subject bibliographies

Subject bibliographies form the largest group of enumerative bibliographies. They are of two kinds:

1 Large-scale *reference* bibliographies
2 Small-scale *reading lists*

Subject bibliographies for reference

In theory there should be exhaustive subject bibliographies. Some large-scale bibliographies appear to be so. But, in fact, it is quite impossible to compile a subject bibliography which is absolutely exhaustive, recording every single publication on its subject, as so much is published which escapes advertisement and legal deposit, and the scattering of contributions to books and periodicals is a problem which defeats even the best bibliographers' vigilance. Also, it must be conceded that there comes a point when no purpose is served by listing a so-called 'contribution' to the literature of a subject simply because it has appeared in print. The large-scale subject bibliographies therefore only aim to be exhaustive within chosen limits, which should be made clear. One common limitation, apart from the exclusion of trivia, is material in some, or all foreign languages.

Large-scale bibliographies can be either *ad hoc* with, perhaps, occasional revision or supplements, or serial bibliographies with the benefit of regular, sometimes frequent publication and time-saving cumulations. Most of the familiar large-scale subject bibliographies are those published serially. They include the indexing and abstracting services discussed in chapter 30.

At their best, non-serial large-scale subject bibliographies are given cover-to-cover revision, but this can be dilatory, or supplements, although several of these can be tiresome to use. Two highly praised bibliographies which have lately been given a new lease of life, one by revision and the other with a supplement, are Leslie T. Morton, *A medical bibliography (Garrison and Morton): An annotated check-list of texts illustrating the history of medicine* (4th edn, Alder-shot: Gower, 1983) and George Ottley, *A bibliography of British railway history* (Allen & Unwin, 1965; reprinted HMSO, 1983; *Supplement* HMSO, 1983).

An interesting group of subject bibliographies which, although mostly used for reference, sometimes encourage browsing when newly published, are the annual biblio-graphical surveys. The object of these is to provide each year classified bibliographies of the more important literature published during a year on particular subjects. Two con-trasting surveys of this kind deal with progress in English studies. They are the *Annual bibliography of English language and literature*, 1921–   (Cambridge University Press for the Modern Language Research Association), a list of books and articles without annotations, and *The year's work in English studies* 1919–   (John Murray for the English Association), a narrative critical survey with the accent on books. For some subjects annual bibliographical surveys are called 'Progress in . . . .'.

Reading lists

Large-scale subject bibliographies are important, especially when they cover more than books. But they are not enough. Anyone who wishes to study a particular subject, at what-ever level, needs a carefully prepared select bibliography of it. Such a bibliography must be appropriate in scale and cautious in its inclusion of out-of-print publications. It must be helpfully arranged and annotated, and reasonably up to date. The more suitable, and more usual name for this kind of bibliography is 'reading list'.

Although reading lists are quite common and produced by people who know or should know the literature they recommend the average standard of reading lists is low. The most lamentable aspect of this is that in the production of reading lists for students in universities, polytechnics, adult education institutes and schools, the subject knowledge of the teachers is seldom linked with the bibliographical know-ledge of the on site librarians. (It should be added that librarians cannot always be depended upon to be biblio-graphically literate, despite their bibliographical instruction at library school.)

When the inadequacy of academic reading lists was ventil-ated by Mike Cornford in the *Library Association Record* a few years ago, the comments published on his article were remarkably unhelpful. One correspondent said that students ought to know from their lectures what their tutors meant by the cryptic references in their reading lists. If not they should ask for clarification. In other words, if a reading list is worth doing, never mind if it is done badly. There are librarians and staffs in bookshops who wince every time they are presented with reading lists emanating from schools, colleges and universities. As I have discussed the need for what I call 'bibliographical literacy' in chapter 37, I will not deal with the all too common faults in reading lists here, although undoubtedly they waste millions of hours in libraries and bookshops. A simple fact of life is that teachers are the most difficult people to convert. What they do they do. To be fair, there are a few exceptions to the general run of amateurish, uninformative, unimaginative and generally frustrating reading lists which add to the burdens of students of all ages. Although they are not beyond criticism, those distributed by the Open University are well above average.

So far I have had in mind reading lists prepared and distributed by tutors. But a further problem with reading lists is that many are provided by the authors of textbooks. They commonly appear at the ends of textbooks under the heading 'Further reading'. These reading lists may not only be poorly compiled, but as their revision has to await the reprinting, probably the revision, of the texts, they, too, are of doubtful value. Generally speaking, publishers are as little concerned with the quality of reading lists in the textbooks they publish as they are with the indexes to them.

An interesting technical point about reading lists at large is that they can be produced in narrative form, like *The year's work in English studies* mentioned earlier in this chapter. This device is not ideal for quick reference (a good reading list is one which, having been read, will thereafter be constantly referred to) but it does encourage students to go through it and it helps the compiler, if he knows what he is doing, to link one publication with another. Good examples (at least they were when they were new) are the reading lists appended to the individual volumes of the *Oxford history of England*. Some of the miniature subject bibliographies in the British Council's *British Book News* (monthly) could be regarded as reading lists. Needless to say, these lists are not only compiled by experts, but the editor of *British Book News* sees to it that they are bibliographically literate.

Further reading

Although it is not up to date, the following bibliography of subject bibliographies is still worth looking at as it gives a good idea of the kind of work subject bibliographers do: Robert L. Collison, *Bibliographies: subject and national* (3rd edn, Crosby Lockwood, 1968).

Two distinguished bibliographers have reflected on the problems of compiling subject bibliographies:

Walford, A.J. 'The plight of the subject bibliographer', *Library Review, 17* (134), Summer 1960, pp.403–8. Ottley, George, 'Tracking the railways', *Library Review, 20* (3), Autumn 1965, pp.163–7.

On the characteristic faults in academic reading lists see Mike Cornford 'Let's make reading lists readable', *Library Association Record, 82* (3), March 1980, p.123 and the ensuing correspondence on pp.191, 331 and 379. For excellent advice on how to compile really helpful reading lists see T. Baum, 'Reference lists for students', *Programmed Learning and Educational Technology, 17* (3), August 1980, pp.175–6.

34 Literature guides

A literature guide is a guide to the literature of a particular subject (for example, mathematics) or broad area of knowledge (for example, science and technology). Its purpose is to give readers concerned with that subject, or group of subjects, the ability to discover information for themselves. No one who studies a subject in depth should be ignorant of the nature and variety of information sources on it.

Some years ago, the late Dr E.J. Crane, long-serving editor of *Chemical Abstracts*, realised that universities and colleges were turning out graduates in chemistry who were unable to make the best use of the libraries of chemical literature available to them when they obtained jobs. Crane therefore devised and compiled, with the help of two associates, a pioneer *Guide to the literature of chemistry*. It was first published in 1927 and for many years was the standard guide to chemical literature. Since 1927 literature guides on many other subjects have appeared, including physics, biology, economics, psychology, medicine, the Victorian age and patents. Some publishers have launched series of literature guides, for example, the 'How to find out' series of the Pergamon Press (now in need of revision) and the rather more erudite 'Use of' series, all of which are symposia, published by Butterworths.

A very good example of a broad based literature guide is one which has been recommended several times in the 'Further reading' sections of this manual, namely, Denis Grogan, *Science and technology: an introduction to the literature* (4th edn, Bingley, 1982). The author states that this guide was written 'primarily for students, not practitioners'.

A literature guide is not a subject bibliography, although it is akin to it. Its primary purpose is to explain how the information on a given subject is packaged. Until recently this meant identifying and commenting upon the various kinds of printed publications. But for most subjects it is now necessary to go beyond these. Secondly, it is necessary to describe and assess all the major sources. Beyond that, only representative examples are necessary, otherwise the reader is faced with wearisome, meaningless lists of sources, and the value of the guide as a teaching tool is lost.

The fact that some very good literature guides fail to reach a second edition, or are revised only at long intervals, suggests that they are not recommended by tutors to their students as they should be. It is a wonder that so many academic projects, theses and dissertations are brought to completion.

Some academic libraries, with or without the aid of the teaching staff, have compiled and distributed their own small-scale literature guides, geared to their own stocks, a practice to be commended.

As usual, there are problems. Some subjects are still not covered by literature guides, and those that are may not have guides suitable for all potential users. A literature guide can be for a practitioner, an intending practitioner (that is a student), an interested amateur or a librarian who will not be actively concerned with the subject itself, but needs to know the literature about it. This point illustrates one of the axioms of librarianship, that a subject is not adequately represented in a library until the sources of information on it meet the needs of all types of readers using the library who are interested in that subject.

A warning is necessary here. A publication calling itself *A guide to the literature of X* may be no more than an annotated list, or even a bare list of publications. The former may be of some use as a bibliography, but it is not really a guide. The best literature guides not only explain, to the uninitiated the nature and uses of periodical literature, microforms, bibliographies, online databases and other sources whose characteristics are not common knowledge, but will include advice on how to use the appropriate libraries.

The long-standing need for a guide to the literature of librarianship has now been met by Ray Prytherch, *Sources of information in librarianship and information science* (Aldershot: Gower, 1983). For recent material see *Cablis*, monthly bulletin of the British Library, Library Association Library.

Further reading

There is not much to read on literature guides in general. But on those in science and technology (which are better provided with literature guides than the social sciences and the humanities) see *Grogan*, chapter 2 'Guides to the literature'. A number of good literature guides are in *Walford*, but not the latest.

35 Author bibliographies

An aspect of bibliographic control of peculiar interest is the bibliography of individual authors. For most authors nothing more than 'title-a-line' lists of their books are likely to be wanted. But for authors of distinction, more especially those of literary distinction, complete and fully descriptive bibliographies are wanted. Notwithstanding that the demand for them is limited to a few types of user, their number has grown considerably over the past thirty years. It is now possible to publish a full-scale bibliography of an author of popular light fiction, such as Edgar Wallace. We have reached the point where we need separate bibliographies of author bibliographies.

As a group, author bibliographies have not received much attention. But individually they have been subjected to meticulous assessment in the review sections of the bibliographical journals, for example *The Library*. From this kind of searching scrutiny few author bibliographers survive unscathed, as perfection in author bibliography is hard to achieve. This observation may come as a surprise. One would expect the bibliographies of authors who lived when new books were listed only in roughly compiled book-trade bibliographies, and periodical indexing services did not exist, to be difficult to compile with absolute precision. But for reasons to be explained later, it is very difficult to compile impeccable bibliographies of twentieth century authors.

Another matter for surprise to those who are unfamiliar with full-scale author bibliographies is their size. A bibliography of an author of even modest industry, such as Sir Max Beerbohm, makes quite a substantial volume.

The obvious question is 'Who wants author bibliographies?'. They are produced mainly for book collectors and members of the antiquarian book-trade. But they can be useful also to biographers and critics. The needs of the latter, who are bound to be interested in the state of the text of a book, which a printer may have corrupted (for example, a Shakespeare quarto), or the author has revised (for example, an early novel by Henry James) is usually regarded as of less importance than the physical 'points' beloved of collectors, who like to gloat over rarities, and invest in them. ('In the first edition, first state, the cover is smooth royal blue cloth and the publisher's Autumn 1908 catalogue is bound in with the text.')

A good author bibliography must be exhaustive in coverage, fully informative in its individual entries, helpfully arranged, and 100 per cent accurate. Although its prime purpose is to list the writings of an author, it sometimes lists also those written about him, but almost certainly many of these will not be worth the trouble. Even the most highly praised biographies and critical studies, unfortunately, are unlikely to survive the generation in which they were published, and writings about an author may continue long after there is no more to publish by the author himself.

Exhaustive coverage means listing every single publication, however trivial, and also, if possible, the author's surviving manuscripts. As most modern authors have published a good deal more than books, tracing all their publications is almost certain to be painfully difficult. This is because of several enduring weaknesses in the pattern of bibliographic control, among them the inadequate coverage by indexing services of newspapers, local periodicals, literary periodicals and authors' contributions to books, such as miscellanies, reference works, and introductions to books by other authors. A good case history is that of G.K. Chesterton (1874–1936), an author of great productivity and versatility, who never blotted a line and never said 'No' to an editor. The standard bibliography of G.K.C., by the late John Sullivan, is in three volumes: *G.K. Chesterton: A bibliography* (University of London Press, 1958); *Chesterton continued: a bibliographical supplement* (University of London Press, 1968) and *Chesterton three: a bibliographical postscript* (Bedford: Vintage Publications, 1980). In both volumes two and three Sullivan had to include additions and corrections to his first volume, which he probably hoped would be definitive.

It is fashionable now to compile bibliographies of living authors, but a bibliographer who thinks that consultation with his subject will solve all or most of his problems must expect to be disappointed. The historian A.J.P. Taylor was able to tell his bibliographer the names of the periodicals and newspapers to which he had contributed, but it required much tedious scanning of their indexes or pages to find these contributions. The resultant work, Chris Wrigley,

157

A.J.P. Taylor: A complete annotated bibliography and guide to his historical and other writings (Brighton: Harvester Press, 1980) is most impressive, but up to its cut-off date is it really complete?

Arundell Esdaile said that a good author bibliography tells a story. It will do so best when, like Wrigley's bibliography, it is generously annotated and the annotations include information on the texts. A classic example of this kind of author bibliography, although it now needs updating, is Stuart Mason, *Bibliography of Oscar Wilde* (T. Werner Laurie, 1914; reprinted Bertram Rota, 1967).

The arrangement of author bibliographies is a matter for argument. Strict chronological order of publication has the merit of indicating, more or less, an author's development. But when applying an author bibliography to the catalogues and shelves of libraries and bookshops, arrangement by physical form is better. The basic formula used by the admirable series of bibliographies of twentieth century British and American authors called 'Soho bibliographies' (originally published by Rupert Hart-Davis, but currently by the Oxford University Press) is as follows:

A   Books and pamphlets
B   Contributions to books
C   Contributions to periodicals
D   Translations
E   Manuscripts

Not all author bibliographies are of famous literary authors. Subject authors, such as Robert Boyle and Florence Nightingale, also have full-scale bibliographies. Furthermore, not all author bibliographies are published as separate volumes. Some are concealed in books, such as the excellent bibliography of the poet Edward Thomas in Robert P. Eckert, *Edward Thomas: A biography and a bibliography* (Dent, 1937). A number of useful small-scale author bibliographies have been published in periodicals, for example the series on minor authors of note published in the *Book Collector* during the 1960s under the collective title 'Some uncollected authors'.

Further reading

There is not a great deal to read on author bibliographies generally, but A.E. Day 'Author bibliographies', *Library*

Review, 21 (2), Summer 1967, pp.81–3 is recommended, more especially because after it was written Day dared to compile an author bibliography himself, *J.B. Priestley: An annotated bibliography* (New York: Garland Publishing, 1980). On the 'Soho bibliographies' see the anonymous survey of the early volumes, 'The Soho recipe', *The Times Literary Supplement*, 25 October 1963, p.876.

36 Records of research in process

Research reports and theses are fundamentally alike: they are all accounts of research which has been done, although not necessarily taken as far as it could be.

The tide of research is an ever-flowing tide, and with a record number of academic, governmental and privately funded research institutions, it flows ever more strongly. For obvious reasons it is desirable to know not only what research has been done, but what research is being undertaken.

Although there are registers of research in progress, they do not cover all subjects, and those that do exist are probably all incomplete. This is because individual researchers are apt to be negligent in reporting their work and in the interests of national security some research activities cannot be made known. The situation is best in science and technology; it is worst in the humanities.

The major British register of research is *Research in British universities, polytechnics and colleges*, vol. 1 *Physical sciences*; vol. 2 *Biological sciences*; vol. 3 *Social sciences* (which also covers government departments and other institutions), British Library Lending Division, 1978–   , published annually. These volumes are broad alphabetical subject lists with name and keyword indexes.

A good small-scale example is *Current research in library and information science*, Library Association, 1983–   , published quarterly. It is the successor to the LA's *RADIALS Bulletin*. The scope of this new register has been extended beyond the UK.

Further reading

Grogan, chapter 19 'Theses and research in progress'.

37 The need for bibliographical literacy

Before taking leave of bibliographies it is necessary to pay some attention to the virtues, and all too common defects, of bibliographical citation. I have not provided a detailed code of bibliographical citation. As there are several standard codes, this is unnecessary. A very good one for student librarians (it is inexpensive and well worth buying) is the *MHRA style book: notes for authors, editors and writers of dissertations*, details of which will be found at the end of this chapter. There is also the handier, but rather terse British Standard, BS 5605 : 1978, *Citing publications by bibliographical references*. If all authors only paid attention to either of these, it would be easier for librarians to observe S.R. Ranganathan's fourth law of library science: *Save the time of the reader*. As it is, millions of hours must be wasted by librarians trying to identify books and periodical articles requested by readers who cannot provide adequate details of them, as the citations they have copied were defective. One expects an author who has mastered his subject, and can write with authority and clarity about it, to apply authority and clarity also to his bibliographical citations. But too often one hopes for too much.

To be precise, I am concerned with two things: lists of *references* and *bibliographies* appended to monographs. A simple primer will not need the former, but all educational works (using the term 'educational' in its broadest sense) should have the latter.

The list, or lists, of references should give the precise sources of all significant facts and ideas taken from other publications, whether or not they appear in the text as significant quotations. The bibliography should be a systematically arranged list of all the major sources used, with annotations where necessary. In an educational or instructional work the bibliography will probably take the form of a list of publications on the subject recommended for 'further reading', in which case all items should be annotated, so that the reader can decide whether they are worth buying or borrowing.

The object of this chapter is to draw attention to common

faults in bibliographical citation, in the hope that the readers of this manual will zealously avoid making them themselves. But before doing so it is necessary to identify briefly the major elements of good citation, first for books and then for periodical articles.

Elements in the bibliographic citation of a book

These should include the author's surname; forenames, or the initial letters of them, as stated on the title page; title and sub-title; number of the edition, other than the first; place of publication; publisher; date of publication; number of volumes, if more than one; series title, where applicable; particular chapters or pages the reader should look at, if relevant.

The faults one frequently comes across in the citations of books are these:

1 Corruption of authors' names

This can be puzzling, if not misleading. Either one gets the initial letter of a forename the author uses in full, or *vice versa*. Thus, B. Russell instead of Bertrand Russell, or John Boynton Priestley instead of J.B. Priestley. When bibliographers (and library cataloguers) veer towards the thin edge of madness they tell us about authors called Charles John Huffam Dickens and Thomas Stearns Eliot, with no indication that these authors did not choose to publish under these names.

2 Suppression of publishers' names and places of publication

This is tiresome. Many books and pamphlets published today are not published by the small number of famous publishers who operate from London. Furthermore, the fact that a title is in English does not help. Books are published in English from China to Peru. One can economise by stating 'Place of publication London, except where otherwise stated'. Otherwise the place of publication should be given.

3 No date of publication

For the reprint of a popular classic this is forgivable. For an informational work it is not. A straightforward reprint of a non-fiction work should give the date of the edition re-printed, and the name of the original publisher if there has been a change.

4 No annotation

If an author hopes you will read a book he includes in his bibliography, he should explain why he recommends it. He should provide an annotation anyway to a book with a non-descriptive title. (If you are studying Victorian fiction, why should you read a book called *The violent effigy*?) An annotation can also make clear that although only one chapter in a certain book is relevant to the subject, it is well worth getting hold of.

Elements in the citation of a periodical article

These include the author's surname; forenames, or the initial letters of them, as given in the periodical; title of the article; title of the periodical; volume number; issue number; date of the issue; inclusive pagination; abstract where needed.

With a periodical article, as with a book, there can be corruption of the author's name, and the lack of an annotation (abstract) where one is needed. Other common faults are:

1 Incomplete citations

It is important to provide the volume number, issue number and the exact date of the issue. The suppression of any of these can cause trouble and delay when the article is requested in a library. A library may file a periodical bound or unbound. If the latter, the issue number will be useful. If the periodical is bound there is no guarantee that both the numbers and dates of the volumes will be put on their spines.

2 Careless abbreviation of a periodical's name

It is a temptation to abbreviate the title of a periodical when it is long, but a non-standard abbreviation could be ambiguous and even a standard abbreviation could mystify some readers.

Arrangement of references

References must be in the order in which they occur in the text. They are usually identified by numbers. There is eternal argument as to whether they should appear at the foot of the relevant pages, at the end of the relevant chapters, or together at the end of the book. Readers' preferences cannot be reconciled.

Arrangement of bibliographies

Bibliographies are another matter. They must be in the most helpful order, but this will depend on the forms and subjects of the items included. If a general history of the Victorian age in Britain listed 165 books and articles in periodicals in one sequence, alphabetically by the names of their authors, so that one had to scan the lot to pick out references to primary education, or the Great Exhibition of 1851, who would bother? The list should be classified, beginning with general works, and under each heading books and pamphlets should be listed first, and then periodical articles.

Further reading

As mentioned above, students are advised to get hold of a copy of the *MHRA style book: notes for authors, editors and writers of dissertations* (3rd edn, Modern Humanities Research Association, 1981). This is obtainable from W.S. Maney & Son Ltd, Hudson Road, Leeds LS9 7DL.

The present author has dealt at greater length with bibliographical citation in James G. Ollé, *Library history* (Clive Bingley, 1979) chapter 7 'Preparing a text for submission'.

Appendices

Appendices

1 Principal sources of information on reference material

The object of this appendix is to give details of the major British and American textbooks on, and bibliographies of, reference material. Most of them have been cited in previous chapters.

Textbooks

Higgens, Gavin (ed.), *Printed reference material*, 2nd edn, Library Association, 1984.
A substantial textbook by a team of 19 experts. Most of the twenty-two chapters are on the traditional types of printed reference sources (dictionaries, encyclopedias, periodicals and so on), but there are chapters on 'On-line information retrieval systems' and 'Videotex information systems'. For general courses of reference materials Higgens must be used with discretion, as quite a large number of individual reference sources are described. But as there is an excellent index, the book can be used for reference as well as study. Note that this second edition has not only been revised throughout, but enlarged.
Katz, William A., *Introduction to reference work*, vol. 1: *Basic information sources*, 4th edn, McGraw Hill, 1982.
This American textbook is not so wide in scope as *Higgens*, either with regard to the types of materials discussed, or in the number of examples described. Furthermore, it is geared to the reference resources of North American libraries. But it is an unusually good textbook on reference materials and is deservedly popular. This edition has been substantially revised, with a welcome change in the pattern of the chapters on bibliographies.
Grogan, Denis, *Science and technology: an introduction to the literature*, 4th edn, Bingley, 1982.
This is a well-informed and lucid survey of the main types of information on science and technology. Some matters which could only be dealt with briefly in *Higgens* have chapters to themselves in *Grogan*, for example research reports and conference proceedings. Some pages are uncomfortably

crowded with titles, but throughout the book there are helpful observations on particular types of literature, rather than mere titles. This edition has a substantial chapter on computerised databases.

There are no literature guides equally good on the two other major areas of knowledge, the social sciences and the humanities.

Bibliographies

The standard British and American bibliographies of reference materials, commonly referred to as *Walford* and *Sheehy*, are not so much rivals as complements. Although they are slanted towards their own country's publications, there is some degree of overlap, although this has become less pronounced since *Walford*, which was originally in one volume, has been expanded into three. The present pattern of *Walford* is as follows:

Walford, A.J., *Guide to reference material*, vol. 1: *Science and technology*, 4th edn, Library Association, 1980; vol. 2: *Social and historical sciences, philosophy and religion*, 4th edn, Library Association, 1983; vol. 3: *Generalia, language, the arts and literature*, 3rd edn, Library Association, 1977.

It has been said that 'Walford is to reference as Gray is to anatomy'. It could be argued that Walford's task has been the more onerous, as reference sources change from day to day. As his remarkable *Guide* is a bibliography every librarian should know, a detailed description of it will give place to an earnest plea to examine it. But note that in comparison with *Sheehy* (a) it is arranged by the Universal Decimal Classification, (b) its annotations often cite author-itative reviews, (c) it does not, as yet, refer to online data-bases and databanks, and (d) it is not updated with supple-ments; each volume is completely revised at intervals of approximately six years. Until recently Dr Walford compiled all three volumes, but they are now being handed over to others.

Although the expansion of *Walford* into three volumes increased its value, some libraries and some personal users needed a more select and less expensive bibliography of reference material. This need has now been met in Walford, A.J., *Walford's concise guide to reference material*, Library

Association, 1981. This abridgement of the three-volume *Walford* has 2,500 main entries. The three-volume *Guide* has 17,000. But in both bibliographies additional titles are mentioned in the annotations. The abridgement has been designed 'to cater particularly for the needs of smaller reference libraries and the bibliographical information seeker in general'. How often the *Concise guide* will be revised is not yet known, but it is to be hoped that sales will encourage frequent revision.

Dr Walford has discussed the problems of compiling his major bibliography in A.J. Walford 'Compiling the *Guide to reference material'*, *Journal of librarianship*, *10* (20 April 1978, pp.88–96. There is a well-deserved appreciation of Dr Walford and his two bibliographies by Denis Grogan 'His name is the guide', *Library Association Record*, *82* (6), June 1980, pp.275–6.

Sheehy, Eugene P., (ed.), *Guide to reference books*, 9th edn, Chicago: American Library Association, 1976; *Supplement*, 1980; *Second supplement*, 1982.

The ALA has published a bibliographical guide to reference material since 1902. It is always referred to by the name of its latest editor. Sheehy is the fourth. Originally this bibliography was arranged by the Decimal Classification, but Dewey order has now been replaced by a grouping 'more in keeping with the subject organisation of many libraries and with the content of courses in library schools'.

Like *Walford*, *Sheehy* has an unsatisfactory policy of revision. The formula for *Sheehy* is cover-to-cover revision at rather long intervals. Between the revised editions it is updated by separately published supplements and a half-yearly annotated list of 'Selected reference books' published in the January and July issues of *College and Research Libraries*, the journal of the Association of College and Research Libraries. The first *Supplement* to the current edition of *Sheehy* is a landmark in this famous bibliography's history as it includes references to online databases, both in the main sequence and in a special section.

Guides to new reference sources

Keeping abreast of new and revised reference sources has always been a vexing problem in British libraries. It has become even greater now that many non-print sources of information have come into use. Time must therefore be found to scrutinise the *Bookseller*, the *BNB* and *British Book News*, as well as the catalogues and prospectuses of the publishers who issue important reference works, such as the Oxford University Press and Butterworths. It is worthwhile, also, to look at *Refer*, the journal of the Reference, Special and Information Section of the Library Association, which includes a regular feature 'Reference books you may have missed'. At present *Refer* is published only twice a year, but its undoubted usefulness may lead to more frequent publication.

Librarians in the USA and Canada have the advantage of several very good lists of new and revised reference works in the leading periodicals of librarianship, in addition to helpful reviews of individual works. As the accent is on American publications these lists and reviews are not much used in the UK, but British students of librarianship are advised to look at the meticulous reviews of new and revised reference works which are published in *The Booklist*, a bi-monthly guide to new books published by the American Library Association. The lengthy reviews of encyclopedias, dictionaries, atlases and so on (a few of them British) are most illuminating, although from the point of view of practising librarians they appear some time after these works have been published.

2   A note on copyright

The current copyright law of the United Kingdom is contained in the Copyright Act of 1956. It is not a satisfactory Act and is urgently in need of revision. The situation has changed a good deal since it was passed. Photocopying, then little used, has become widespread and there are several new media presenting new problems. The government is aware that new legislation is necessary and several years ago appointed a committee to investigate the matter. The committee's report, usually referred to as the *Whitford Report*, after the name of the chairman, John Whitford, is officially entitled *Report of the Committee to consider the law on copyright and designs*, Cmnd. 6732 (HMSO, 1977). Since then there has been a Green Paper, *Reform of the law relating to copyright . . . a consultative document*, Cmnd. 8302 (HMSO, 1981), but the only new legislation has been the Copyright Amendment Act, 1983, which deals solely with recording radio and TV.

The copyright law is easily broken, but that is no reason why librarians should break it, or encourage their readers to do so. Fortunately, there are helpful guides to the law as it stands. First, there is a series of clear and concise pamphlets published and distributed by the Council for Educational Technology, 3 Devonshire Street, London W1N 2BA. This is a comprehensive series and deals separately with broadcast programmes, films and computers, as well as printed material.

There is also a good book on copyright, all the more helpful because it has been written by a well-informed librarian for librarians: L.J. Taylor, *Copyright for librarians* (Brighton: Tamarisk Books, 1980). This covers current legislation, the *Whitford Report* and the discussions which have followed it.

On photocopying, which concerns most libraries, see Raymond A. Wall, 'Photocopying rights and wrongs: a librarian's view', *Aslib Proceedings, 34* (2), February 1982, pp.113–28.

Index

abstract journals, 139–42
Acts of Parliament, 28, 71–2
American book publishing record, 121
analytical bibliography, 108
Annual register, 54
anthologies, 67–8
antonyms, dictionaries of, 40
atlases, 88–9
audio, discs and tapes, 18–9
audiovisual materials, 20, 118–9
author bibliographies, 156–8

Baker, E.A. and Packman, J.A., *Guide to the best fiction*, 147
Benn's press directory, 130–1
Besterman, Theodore, *World bibliography of bibliographies*, 111–2
bibliographic control, 108–110
Bibliographic index, 113
bibliographical citation, 111–2, 161–4
bibliographical literacy, 161–4
bibliographies
annotated, 163
arrangement, 164
assessment of, 111–2

author, 156–8
bibliographies of, 113
national, 115–124
newspapers, 129–132
periodicals, 129–132
subject, 149–152
bibliography, definition of, 108
Bibliography of British newspapers, 57
biographical information
biographical dictionaries, 81–4
biographical quotations, 96
miscellaneous sources, 81, 83–4
Biography index, 84
BLAISE-LINE, 26, 29, 128
BLAISE-LINK, 26
Booklist, 170
books
bibliographies of, 115–118
Xerox copies, 16
Books in English, 122
Books in print, 121–2
Britain: an official handbook, 54
Britannica year book, 49
British book news, 119
British catalogue of audiovisual materials, 20
British catalogue of music, 118
British government publications
bibliographies of, 72–3
catalogues, 72

172

HMSO publications,
  71–2
non-HMSO publications,
  72,
subject scope, 71–2
British humanities index,
  136
British Institute of Recorded
  Sound, 19
British Library
  Bibliographic Services
    Division, 117–120,
    124
  Lending Division, 103,
    132, 144, 160
  Library Association
    Library, 103
  National Sound Archive,
    19
  Newspaper Library, 55,
    57–8
  Reference Division, 126
*British Museum Library
  catalogue*, 126, 131
*British national biblio-
  graphy (BNB)*
  bibliographies in, 113
  general description,
    117–8
  cataloguing-in publica-
    tion (CIP), 120
  periodicals in, 131
British Standards Institution
  (BSI), 93
British technology index,
  136
*British union catalogue of
  periodicals* (BUCOP),
  60, 131
bulletins, library, 142

cable TV, 32
Cablis, 103

*Catalogue of scientific
  papers*, 136
catalogues of libraries,
  published
  history of, 125
  national, 126
  special, 127
  union, 127–8
cataloguing-in-publication
  (CIP), 118, 120
Central Statistical Office,
  75–7
Chemical abstracts, 25,
  142
Choice, 122
collections of writings
  anthologies, 67–8
  Festschriften, 67–8
  original, 66–7
  previously published,
    66–7
Collier's encyclopedia, 50
Collison, Robert L.
  on catalogues, 125
  on bibliographies, 112
  on microforms, 31
*Columbia Lippincott
  gazetteer*, 90
compact discs, 19
concealed bibliographies,
  37, 111
concordances, 96–7
conference proceedings
  bibliographic control,
    144–5
  uses, 65
copyright
  general, 171
  international, 5
  Ordnance Survey maps,
    87
Cumulated fiction index,
  147

Cumulative book index (CBI), 121—3
current awareness bulletins, 142
Current British journals, 130—1
Current contents series, 138
Current research in library and information science, 160
Current technology index, 136

databanks, 27—8
databases, 26—7
dictionaries, language
  abbreviations, 39
  American, 41
  choice of, 41—2
  defining, 38—9
  encyclopedic, 39
  English, 38—42
  foreign language, 42
  learners', 39
  slang, 40
  thesauri, 41
dictionaries, subject
  biographical, 81—4
  quotations, 95—6
  small subject encyclopædias, 51—2
Dictionary of national biography, 82—3
directories, 78—80
Directory of title-pages, indexes and contents pages, 134
dissertations, 102—3
document delivery, 27—8, 141
document transmission, 27

Eighteenth-century short-title catalogue (ESTC), 26, 128

Einbinder, Harvey, *Myth of the Britannica,* 48—9
electronic periodicals, 64
Encyclopædia Britannica, 47—9, 54
encyclopedias
  general, 47—50, 81
  large-scale, 47—50
  small-scale, 51—2
  subject, 50—2
Encyclopedia Americana, 49—50
Encyclopedia of library and information science, 51
Engineering index, 142
English catalogue of books, 115
English historical documents series, 67
English literature, bibliographies of, 112, 146—7
enumerative bibliography, 108
ephemera, printed, 100—101
Essay and general literature index, 67
Europa year book, 54

Festschriften, 67—8
fiction, bibliographies of, 147—8
forms of information sources, 2
Forthcoming books, 122
Future of the printed word, 32—4

Gaselee, Sir Stephen, 31
GATEWAY, 22
gazetteers, 89—90
geographical sources of information
  atlases, 88—9
  gazetteers, 89—90

maps, 85—8
  Ordnance Survey of
    Great Britain, 87—9,
    91
Good book guide, 119
government publications
  American, 73
  British, 71—3
  catalogues of, 70—3
  characteristics of, 70—1
  marketing of, 70—1
  microform reprints, 15
  scope of, 69, 71
gramophone records, 18—19
Granger's index to poetry,
  148
Grogan, Denis, *Science and
  technology: an introduction to the literature*,
  168—9
Guide to official statistics,
  76

*Harrap's new standard
  French-English dictionary*,
  42
Harrod, L.M., *Librarian's
  glossary*, 40
Her Majesty's Stationery
  Office (HMSO), 71—3
Higgens, Gavin, *Printed
  reference material*, 168
Hunt Report on cable TV,
  32

illustrations, 98—9
Index medicus, 135
*Index of conference pro-
  ceedings received*, 144
*Index to scientific and
  technical proceedings*,
  144—5
Index to theses, 103
Indexer, 44

information technology, 31
*International books in
  print*, 123
Internatioanl Standard
  Book Numbers, 116
International Standard
  Serial Numbers, 129

Katz, William A., *Introduction to reference work*,
  168
*Keesing's contemporary
  archives*, 56
KINGTEL, 24

legal deposit, 60, 118
legal information, online,
  27—8
librarianship, bibliographies
  of
  Cablis, 154
  *Current research in
    library and informa-
    tion science*, 160
  *Index to Festschriften
    in librarianship*, 68
  *Library and information
    science abstracts
    (LISA)*, 141
  Library literature, 36
  Radials bulletin, 160
  *Sources of information
    in librarianship and
    information science*,
    154
librarianship, reference
  works on
  Copyright for librarians,
    172
  *Encyclopedia of library
    and information
    science*, 51
  *Harrod's librarian's
    glossary*, 40

Librarian's handbook,
67
*Library and information
science abstracts (LISA)*,
141
Library Association, Information Technology Group,
34
Library literature, 137, 141
Line, Maurice B.
  on bibliographical searches,
  26
  on document delivery,
  27
  on print versus non-print,
  33
literary forms of sources of
information, 2
literature, bibliographies of,
153–4
literature guides, 153–4
local government publications, 73
*London bibliography of the
social sciences*, 127

Macmillan encyclopedia, 51
manuscripts, 16
maps, 85–8
MEDLINE, 135
microforms
  bibliographic control, 17
  disadvantages, 15–16
  future of, 31
  microcards, 15
  microfiches, 15
  microfilm, 14, 55
  Microprint, 15
  uses of, 15–16
monographs, 44–6

national bibliographies
  American, 121–2
  British, 119–20

history of, 115
National Grid, 88
National Library of Wales,
  Microfiche catalogue,
  126–7
National Sound Archive, 19
National union catalog,
  127
*New Cambridge bibliography
  of English literature*, 132,
  146
New Caxton encyclopædia,
  50
*New Grove dictionary of
  music and musicians*, 51
*New Oxford illustrated
  dictionary*, 39
newspapers
  *Bibliography of British
  newspapers*, 57
  British Library Newspaper
  Library, 55, 57–8
  history of, 55
  indexes, 56
  microform copies, 55
  newspaper cuttings, 57
  talking newspapers, 18
  uses, 55, 57

Obituaries from The Times,
  84
official publications, *see*
  government publications
online
  definition of, 25
  disadvantages, 26–7
  uses, 25–8, 110
oral history, 18
Ordnance Survey of Great
  Britain, 87–9, 91
*Oxford dictionary of
  quotations*, 95
Oxford English dictionary,
  39–40

Partridge, Eric, *Dictionary
of slang*, 40
patent specifications, 92–3
Patents Information Net-
work (PIN), 93
periodicals
abstracts, 139–42
citation indexes, 128
contents lists, 127–8
directories of, 129–131
electronic, 64
history, 60
house journals, 59
indexes, 134, 138
library problems with,
60–1
little magazines, 59
microform copies of,
60, 131
uses, 61–2
Victorian, 62–3, 131–2
physical forms of sources
of information, 2
picture librarianship, 98–9
*Poole's index to periodical
literature*, 135
PRESTEL, 22–3
printed word
future of, 29, 31–4
history of, 11–13
Prytherch, Ray
Librarian's glossary, 40
*Sources of information
in librarianship*, 154

quotations, dictionaries
of, 95–7

Ranganathan, S.R., 3, 161
reading lists, 112, 150–1
Refer, 72, 171
reference materials,
bibliographies of, 169
manuals on, 168–9

varieties of, 1–3
references, bibliographical,
164
research, registers of, 160
Research Society for
Victorian Periodicals, 62
Rodgers, Frank, *Guide to
British government
publications*, 72–3
Roget, P.M., *Thesaurus of
English words and
phrases*, 21
Royal Society of London,
scientific bibliographies
by, 136

Science citation index, 138
Sequels, 147
Sheehy, Eugene P., *Guide
to reference books*, 113,
170
*Short-title catalogue:
eighteenth century
(ESTC)*, 26, 128
*Short-title catalogue 1475–
1640 (STC)*, 127
*Short-title catalogue 1641–
1700 (Wing)*, 128
Smith, F.S., *An English
library*, 112
Soho bibliographies series,
158
standards, 93–4
Standing Committee on
Official Publications
(SCOOP), 53–4
Statesman's year book,
53–4
statistics
bibliographies of, 76–7
British government, 75–6
international, 76
online, 27
primary, 74

secondary, 74, 76
unpublished, 75
videotex, 24
Statutes, 28, 71–2
Statutory Instruments, 28, 72
subject bibliographies, 149–52
Subject guide to forthcoming books, 122
Subject index to periodicals 136
Sullivan, John, *G.K. Chesterton: A bibliography*, 157
systematic bibliography, 108
synonyms, dictionaries of, 40

Taylor, A.J.P., 78, 158
Taylor, L.J.
Copyright for librarians, 172
Librarian's handbook, 67
telephone directories, 78
teletext, 22
television, cable, 32
theses, bibliographies of, 102–3
Times atlas of the world, 89–90
Times index, 56, 58
Times obituaries, 84
titles of books, 45
treatises, 44

Ulrich periodical directories, 129
Unesco, bibliographical work of, 110, 115–6
United Kingdom Serials Group, 63–4
United Nations statistical year book, 76

universal bibliographic control (UBC), 123
Urquhart, D.J., 44–5

Victorian periodicals
bibliographies of, 131–2
indexes of, 62–3
uses, 62
video, 20, 93
videotex, 22–4
viewdata, 22
visual aids, 20–1, 118–9

Walford, A.J., *Guide to reference material*, 113, 169–170
Waterloo directory of Victorian periodicals, 131–2
Webster English dictionaries, 90
Weekly record, 121
Wellesley index to Victorian periodicals, 135
Whitaker & Son, bibliographies of British books, 117, 119–20
Whitaker's almanack, 53
Whitford Report on copyright, 172
Who was who, 83
Who's who, 83
Willing's press guide, 130–1
Wilson, H.W., bibliographies
books, 121
periodical literature, 135, 137
Wing, Donald, *Short-title catalogue 1641–1700*, 128
Wintle, Justin and Richard Kenin, *Dictionary of biographical quotation*, 96

yearbooks, 53–4